Curiosities Series

New Mexico
CURIOSITIES

Quirky characters, roadside oddities & other offbeat stuff

Sam Lowe

Guilford, Connecticut

The prices, rates, and hours listed in this guidebook were confirmed at press time. We recommend, however, that you call establishments to obtain current information before traveling.

To buy books in quantity for corporate use
or incentives, call **(800) 962–0973**
or e-mail **premiums@GlobePequot.com.**

Cover photos by the author except vintage toys, curio box © Shutterstock
Interior photos by the author unless otherwise noted; vintage toys © Shutterstock.
Text design by Bret Kerr
Layout by Joanna Beyer
Maps © Morris Book Publishing, LLC

Library of Congress Cataloging-in-Publication Data
Lowe, Sam.
  New Mexico curiosities : quirky characters, roadside oddities & other offbeat stuff / Sam Lowe.
      p. cm. — (Curiosities series)
  ISBN 978-0-7627-4670-5
  1. New Mexico—Miscellanea. 2. Curiosities and wonders—New Mexico. I. Title.
  F796.L68 2009
  978.9—dc22

                                                                        2008042750

Printed in the United States of America

10 9 8 7 6 5 4 3 2 1

To my wife, Lyn, who slipped love notes into my travel bags and listened to my stories about UFOs, ghost towns, Billy the Kid, and weird rock formations.

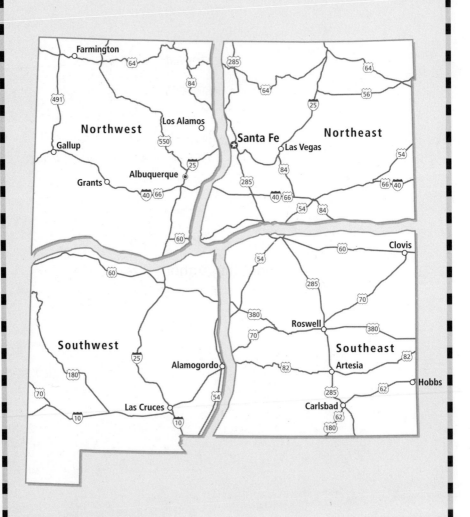

Farmington
64
84
285
64
64
491
Northwest
Los Alamos
Santa Fe
Northeast
550
Gallup
Las Vegas
56
25
25
Albuquerque
84
54
Grants
40 66
285
66 40
40 66
60
54 84
60
Clovis
60
54
Southwest
285
60
70
380
60
Roswell
380
70
25
70
Southeast
180
82
Alamogordo
82
Artesia
70
285
Hobbs
62
10
Las Cruces
Carlsbad
62
10
54
180

New Mexico

contents

introduction

★ ★

This is from my heart.

Over the years I always figured there'd be things in New Mexico that I'd like. It was a sense that spending time there would enrich me. And now, having spent about 15 percent of a full year and driving almost 10,000 miles across and around the state, I find that my initial hunch was correct. New Mexico is indeed the Land of Enchantment.

From Lordsburg to Clayton, from Jal to Shiprock, from Hobbs to Albuquerque, and Chama to Las Cruces, my inquiries were greeted with smiles and genuine offers to help. A bank president in Truth or Consequences conducted a minitour to point out a rock formation that looks like a giant turtle. A newspaper publisher in Carrizozo gave explicit directions to a structure that looks like a giant spider. A waitress in Santa Rosa made sure I got to a scuba divers' hangout in the middle of the high desert. A ranger at Carlsbad Caverns patiently explained how to tell a stalagmite from a stalactite.

My wanderings took me into visitor centers, chambers of commerce, museums, art galleries, souvenir shops, alien spaceship landing sites, prehistoric ruins, and, occasionally, if all else failed, a local saloon or two. Before my fact-finding journey began, I was already aware of some of the curious things I'd find in New Mexico. Like Roswell. And that mysterious spiral staircase in the chapel in Santa Fe. Like Ham the Space Chimp. And Smokey Bear and the giant roadrunners.

But while fulfilling the ambition to see more of New Mexico while seeking things of a curious nature, I also came across men who create sculptures out of washing machine parts and beer bottles, an artist who sponsors a festival for painted burros, a woman who collected Avon bottles, and a man who salvages old windmills. And every one of them, plus hundreds of others, willingly and gladly shared their stories.

Because of their sincerity, and because of New Mexico's spectacular scenery, I will return many times, even though my work there is finished. This journey is over, but many others await me in a land where a handshake and a smile are as common and as enduring as the setting sun.

vi

Signs of the Times

New Mexicans utilize an interesting variety of signs to get their messages across.

- One of the more impressive sits on a sidehill just north of Fort Wingate. It's a smiley face and the words STAY DRUG FREE. The sign is about 40 feet high and the creators used rocks to fashion the face and the message. Then, to make sure it doesn't go unnoticed, they painted every rock bright orange.

- Pay attention to this one: A sign along a pathway at the Salinas Pueblo Missions National Monument reads: RESPECT THE RATTLESNAKE'S PRIVACY. PLEASE STAY ON THE TRAIL.

- Even more ominous is the sign posted at a rest stop near Las Cruces. It warns, simply but effectively: BEWARE OF SNAKES. That'll get your attention in a hurry.

- Off to the left of the front door at the Tucumcari Historical Museum sits a piece of white wood with a bear trap attached to it. The bear trap has been painted red. The wording above it reads: THIS IS NOT A TOURIST TRAP.

- Those who stop in White Oaks can buy a tee shirt advertising the No Scum Allowed Saloon, a popular watering hole.

- A warning on the menu in Tia Sophia's, a downtown Santa Fe restaurant, cautions patrons: "Not Responsible for Too Hot Chile."

- A warning to those who take a dirt road leading to an oil rig along Highway 18 south of Hobbs: SPEED LIMIT 20 MPH. IF A DUST CLOUD IS FOLLOWING YOU, DAMN IT, YOU ARE GOING TOO FAST.

1

Northeast

Ah, northeastern New Mexico, *one of my favorite places. It's a land where blue elephants coexist with blue jackalopes and empty beer bottles are given new life as construction material by artists and home builders. It is a landscape covered with tall pines, quirky houses, and wooden bears. And it has a history alive with tales of gunmen, prehistoric men, cement men, and men who used tractor seats to create less-than-monumental yard sculptures.*

It was in northeastern New Mexico that I met my first ductosaurus, a rather forlorn creature. And it was here that I ran my fingers along the steps of an intricate circular staircase which, depending upon whose story you believe, was built either by St. Joseph or a more earthly woodworker.

Had I brought a swimsuit along on my journey through this enchanting area, I could have gone scuba diving in the northeastern desert. Had I brought a supersensitive hearing aid along, I might have listened to the infamous Taos Hum. Both eluded me because of my lack of preparation, but I did see with my own eyes a dragon peeking its head out of a field of alfalfa, so I do not feel cheated.

Equally impressive were the folks I met along the way. They offered food, information, tall tales, gossip, actual fact and, most importantly, none of them flinched when I asked them if they knew where to find the world's largest collection of belly button lint.

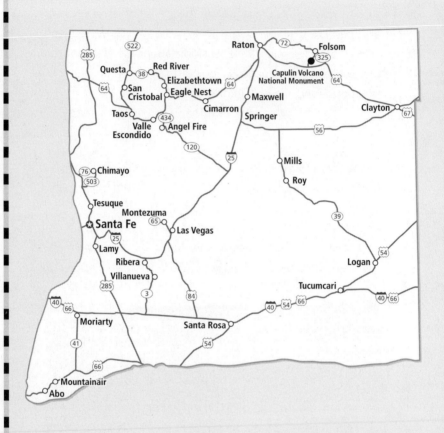

Northeast

★ ★

Aren't Those Things Supposed to Be Pink?
Abo

Here an elephant stands alongside the road, mournfully watching the traffic pass by. It's basic blue with splotches of yellow, red, and green. This would seem to be a direct violation of the elephant color code because, as all veterinarians, zoologists and overimbibers know, elephants normally come only in gray or pink.

A couple of other factors also hint that it probably isn't a real elephant. For one thing it's been standing in that exact same spot for more than forty years. For another thing it's made of cement. And, as a clincher, it's only about 4 feet tall at the shoulders instead of the usual elephant size, which is generally somewhere between huge and "Holy head cold! Did you see the snout on that thing?!!!"

A lonely blue elephant stands guard
on the roadside near Abo.

★ ★

The creature appears to be standing guard at a structure that once served as a restaurant. It was allegedly placed there in the 1960s by a former owner of the property as the result of losing an election bet. Details are sketchy, but according to one source, the principals involved were on different sides of the political fence. In other words, one was a Democrat and the other a Republican. They agreed that whoever lost the bet had to put a symbol of the other guy's party on his property. A Republican won the election so the Democrat had to install the elephant. Had it turned out the other way, there'd be a cement donkey standing lonely vigil somewhere in the area.

Or so the story goes. Psychedelic pachyderm proponents who want to see it to believe it will spot the creature on the north side of U.S. Highway 60, about seven miles west of Mountainair.

Here, Snowee Snowee Snowee
Angel Fire

When November rolls around and the sun's route wanders farther to the south, it is time for the Calling of the Snow, an unofficial function that marks the beginning of the ski season in the southern Rockies of northern New Mexico. The event is held in the parking lot of the Angel Fire Resort and is, according to the people who staff the Tourist Information Center, designed to "invoke the snow gods to give us enough snow for a good ski season."

Participants compete in such categories as loudest call and most unusual call. In the past they have used old brass English horns and kazoos to help their appeals to the gods of the white stuff. One contestant showed up with a huge alpen horn; others have used compressed air horns. And yes, some of them actually do holler, "Snowee! Here, Snowee!" when it comes their turn.

The callers and hollerers get backup support from snow chanters, the beat of snow drums, and the rhythm of snow dances. Winners are awarded nominal prizes but the big reward comes with the knowledge that their pleas for white powder will be answered. Snow has fallen every year since the event began. Of course, it also fell every year *before* the event began.

While all that is going on, resort workers ignite a big bonfire and burn an 8-foot effigy of a golfer because the golfing season is over and now it's time for skiing, snowboarding, quaffing rum nog, and other winter sports. And then everybody gathers round the fire to make S'mores.

Angel Fire is about 28 miles east of Taos on U.S. Highway 64, then two miles south on Highway 434. Snow callers and others who wish to cleanse their lungs by yelling into the pure mountain air can get more information by calling (800) 633-7463 or logging onto www .angelfireresort.com.

A Monumental Tribute

Angel Fire

The Vietnam Veterans National Memorial emerges dramatically and gracefully from the side of a small mountain just north of the Angel Fire turnoff on US 64, some 28 miles east of Taos. The 6,000-square-foot shrine honors the men and women who served in Vietnam and was the first state park in the country dedicated solely to their memory.

The memorial was established in 1968 by Dr. Victor and Jeanne Westphall to honor their son, Lt. David Westphall, who was killed in Vietnam earlier that year. The facility opened in 1971 and since then has drawn almost three million visitors.

The small nondenominational chapel on the grounds has curving walls that converge on a tall window where visitors can look out into the peace of Moreno Valley below. Or they can use the available seating space to meditate while the textured interior surfaces capture the sunlight and cast subtle colorations across the walls. The chapel is open 24 hours a day.

Outside, a bronze life-size sculpture of a soldier reflects upon the madness of war. Nearby, a small plaque on the walkway adds

★ ★

a footnote to the shrine's beginnings. According to this plaque, in 1994, Dr. Westphall gathered a handful of dirt from that spot and took it to Vietnam. There he scattered it at the ambush site where his son was killed, then removed some earth from that scene, brought it back to the memorial, and mixed it with New Mexican soil.

The literature given to visitors emphasizes that the purpose of the memorial "is not to glorify war, but to honor the men and women who served in Vietnam, as well as all veterans for the selfless sacrifices they made at their country's bidding."

The visitor's center includes a display that traces the history of conflict and a special area where veterans can use on-site computers to gather information about the war itself and those with whom they served.

For more information, log onto www.angelfirememorial.com or call (575) 377-6900.

Looking Off into Forever
Capulin Volcano National Monument

There's a belief in these parts that if you stand on the very top of Capulin Volcano National Monument and look north and east, you can see five different states. Well publicized, this assertion is mentioned in many tourist-oriented books about the general area.

According to the folks who claim to know about such things, those who reach the top will be able to see parts of New Mexico, Colorado, Texas, Oklahoma, and Kansas from that vantage point. It's an assumption at best because there's nobody out there in Kansas holding up signs like "Hi, Dorothy. You and Toto hurry back home now, y'hear."

The rangers at the monument don't have too much to say about the allegation, other than an observation that "you have to use some imagination" to look into all five states. New Mexico, of course, is a given. Colorado, less than 50 miles away, is a pretty safe bet. And Texas and Oklahoma are within a 100-mile radius, so with the volcano rising to 8,182 feet above sea level, they're a possibility, particularly on a clear day. But Kansas? One ranger put it this way: "We keep it within the realm of possibility because Kansans get mad at us if we don't."

Capulin volcano's crater is accessible via any one of four trails, which vary in distance and difficulty. The volcano erupted between 56,000 and 62,000 years ago, toward the end of a period of volcanism in the region that began about nine million years ago. The cone consists mainly of loose cinder, ash and other rock debris, and straddles both grasslands and forests.

For those people who want to visit five states without actually going there, the monument is near the small town of Capulin on US 64. Take Highway 325 north out of Capulin for about three miles to the visitor center. And even if you can't see Kansas, the view is spectacular.

You can find the entrance to the park 3 miles north of Capulin on Highway 325. For more information call (575) 278-2201 or log onto www.nps.gov/cavo.

The Holiness of Dirt
Chimayo

Most of the wall space in the sacristy of El Santuario del Chimayo is covered with icons, pictures, and other religious symbols. But one section initially appears to have nothing to do with faith—a row of crutches and braces hanging from racks attached to the wall. The reason for this oddity becomes perfectly clear upon learning about the history and legend of the church.

The small adobe structure is frequently referred to as "The Lourdes of the Southwest" because, like the shrine in France where the faithful believe the Blessed Virgin visited St. Bernadette, it is said to be responsible for miraculous cures. And the crutches and other medical devices here, like those at Lourdes, were placed by those who left their afflictions behind.

★ ★

The stories of the miracles center around a small hole in the ground in a room off to the side of the altar. Many believe that the dirt from the floor of the sanctuary (called *tierra bendita* or "sacred earth") has curative powers, so pilgrims come to remove small portions of the earth from the hole, aided by a couple of small tin shovels left there for such purposes.

The origins of the legend go back to the Tewa Indians, some of the first inhabitants of the area. Later, Spanish settlers propagated the belief that the ground was sacred by recalling miracles, and a shrine was built on the spot in 1758 when an archbishop claimed he had been cured of a contagious disease after a visit.

Around 1810, according to another part of the legend, a friar saw a light bursting from a hillside, dug into the spot and found a crucifix. The icon was taken to a nearby town but it disappeared. This happened two more times until the crucifix was found back in its original site. Believing this to be a sign from above, the people built a small chapel there. Miraculous healings began shortly thereafter at that spot and became so numerous that

Legend says the dirt from the floor of Santuario del Chimayo has wrought miracles.

the chapel had to be replaced by the larger, current Chimayo Shrine. It was built in 1816 and is still very much in its original condition.

Chimayo is located about 40 miles northeast of Santa Fe. Take U.S. Highway 285 north out of Santa Fe to Highway 76, and then drive about four miles east. The little church is in the heart of the community, sitting in a verdant area so beautiful that even skeptics should find a degree of peace there.

The Santuario del Chimayo is about 1 mile south of town on Highway 98. For more information, log on to www.holychimayo.us.

Brother, Can You Spare a Nickel?
Cimarron

Remember when you were growing up and your dad warned, "Be careful not to take any wooden nickels"? Most people never got the opportunity anyway and probably would have accepted one had it been offered. But there's a wooden nickel here that even Dear Old Dad would have loved to acquire, despite his own admonitions to the contrary.

It's 3 feet in diameter. And it's made of wood.

Actually more of a sign than a curio, it sits in the window of the Buffalo Nickel, an art gallery located a block north of US 64, as the highway courses through the village. It was carved specifically to draw attention to the gallery and it does. But it gets some help in the task from a life-size white buffalo statue in an adjacent window.

The gallery/store, whose signage advertises that it also sells "postcards, posters and pickles," has been closed since early 2008 but the owners hope to get it reopened. The nickel is still there, waiting for someone to build a one-armed bandit with a 3-foot slot.

Are You Sure That's Lucien?
Cimarron

A rustic and weather-worn statue of a man wearing a big cowboy hat and an equally big mustache sits on a lot just north of the visitor

information center here. It's undoubtedly folk art because it's concrete, which is the primary medium. The sign below says it's Lucien B. Maxwell, one of the town's more famous residents in the late 1800s.

Toward the end of the 19th century, Maxwell owned a controversial 1.7 million-acre land grant, which he acquired through marriage. It was, and still is, the largest amount of land ever owned by a single individual in the United States. When Maxwell sold the property in 1870, it set off a great deal of controversy and caused a bloody episode known as the Colfax County War, which brought lawlessness, which in turn, brought outlaws into the area.

Maxwell died in 1875 but his statue is still a bone of contention. According to one popular piece of local lore, it was originally commissioned by Henry Springer, an area businessman, to be of himself. But when the artist was finished, Springer didn't like the result and said statues should represent dead people, so they decided the sculpture would be Maxwell instead. Judging from historic photos, it sort of looks like Maxwell, especially the big mustache.

Like so many others in New Mexico's history, Maxwell also had (and still has) a direct connection with Billy the Kid. The house in which Billy met his fate at the hands of Sheriff Pat Garrett was owned by Pete Maxwell, Lucien's son. And Lucien is buried in the same graveyard that holds Billy's mortal remains at Fort Sumner.

The statue is surrounded by a white picket fence and sits 20 steps north of the visitor center, which sits on US 64 about 40 miles south of Raton.

Wild and Woolly
Cimarron

Cimarron means "wild" or "unruly" in Spanish, and twenty-nine bullet holes in the hammered tin ceiling of the St. James Hotel support the idea that it was a suitable name for the town back in the 1880s. Because it was a vital outpost on the old Santa Fe Trail, the St. James was a gathering place for several of history's more unsavory characters, including Jesse James and Bob Ford. This was, obviously, before Ford shot James in the back of the head.

Twenty-six men were killed in or in front of the St. James. One of them was Davy Crockett II, who was mortally wounded in a gunfight on the street that runs past the hotel. Clay Allison also hung out there. A plaque on one wall claims he killed nineteen men and lists them by name, and it's said he also danced naked in the bar and was responsible for several of the bullet holes. Ironically, Allison met his demise when he fell off a freight wagon.

Other famous, or infamous, hotel guests included Buffalo Bill Cody and Annie Oakley, who met in the hotel. Zane Grey, Bat Masterson, Lucien Maxwell, Kit Carson, Billy the Kid, and Henri Lambert, personal chef to President Abraham Lincoln, and, in 1872, founder of the saloon that evolved into the St. James Hotel, all stayed there at one point. They're all gone, of course, but the hotel still welcomes folks to its fourteen rooms.

Guests today are of a gentler demeanor. They eat in the Carson-Maxwell Dining Room and take liquid refreshment in the Lambert Saloon. As sort of a tribute to those wilder times on the frontier, however, there are no television sets or telephones in the rooms. But the tin ceilings have never been repaired so the bullet holes are still there as permanent reminders of a notorious past.

The hotel is located on Highway 21 about ½ mile south of US 64, which serves as the town's main drag. For details call (866) 472-2664 or log onto www.stjamescimarron.com.

How Not to Lose at Poker
Cimarron

What good is an old hotel story if it doesn't involve a ghost or two? The St. James Hotel doesn't disappoint in that genre.

The most famous apparition that supposedly haunts the hotel is allegedly that of T. J. Wright, a guest who won big bucks in a poker game while staying at the establishment. But as he was leaving the poker room, one of the other disgruntled players shot him in the back. Although mortally wounded, Wright was able to stagger back to his room before he died there.

The room was closed after several ghostly disturbances and hasn't been rented out since. But now guests and employees periodically report incidents of a curious nature, like window shades being opened and silverware and glasses flying around the dining area. Apparently, T. J. Wright is still upset about losing his winnings. Ghostbusters and six-shooter shooters alike can get more information at www.stjamescimarron.com or call (505) 376-2664.

Is That a Ductosaurus?
Clayton

There was a time when dinosaurs were big, both literally and figuratively, in this area. Scientists and paleontologists say eight different kinds of the creatures left their footprints in an ancient mudflat more

A replica of an ancient beast has undergone some do-it-yourself repair in Clayton.

than 100 million years ago, and more than 500 of their tracks can still be viewed at Clayton Lake State Park.

Many of the huge reptiles left three-toed tracks, an indication that they were probably ancestors of today's birds. But one left diamond-shaped imprints, similar to those found in China but nowhere else. Some of the most unusual tracks are those of a baby dinosaur and a pterodactyl, the famed flying lizard.

Since the dinosaurs disappeared a long, long, long time ago, maybe even longer ago than that, there aren't any live ones on public display, like in zoos or wild animal parks. But there are replicas. Two of them stand in front of the Clayton/Union County Chamber of Commerce and Tourism Information Center at 1103 South First Street (U.S. Highway 87). Their names are Moonbeam and Spike. There used to be three mini-dinos on the site, but the one known as Raunchy Rex has been mounted on a trailer and now appears only in parades.

But time has also taken its toll on the two impersonators who stand guard at the visitor center. The horns of the triceratops have been pulled away from its head, and one eye has popped out of the creature's skull. In order to heal the damage caused by the elements and young explorers, the curators grafted the loose parts back into their original positions. So now they're held on with the one thing that has helped mankind survive for decades and might even have saved the real dinosaurs from extinction—duct tape.

Clayton is 15 miles west of the Texas border on U.S. Highway 56/412. For more information on dinosaurs and repair jobs, call (800) 390-7858 or log onto www.claytonnewmexico.net.

One Town's Answer to Billy
Clayton

Many New Mexican towns have direct ties to Billy the Kid. Many of those who don't can usually dig up, literally, some other famous bad man that they can claim as their own.

In Clayton it's Thomas "Black Jack" Ketchum, a rather inept criminal who acquired his nickname because he was once mistaken for Gen. John "Black Jack" Pershing. Ketchum and his brother, Sam, had a particular fondness for train robberies, but they weren't particularly good at it. Sam Ketchum was mortally wounded during one attempt in 1899. Only a few days later, while trying to single-handedly hold up another train, Black Jack was wounded by a shotgun blast fired by the conductor. He fled the scene but was apprehended at a waterhole and finally returned to Clayton to stand trial on charges of "felonious assault upon a railroad train." The charge carried a death penalty and Ketchum was hanged on April 26, 1901, shortly after telling his cell mates, "I'll be in hell before you start breakfast, boys."

But his troubles didn't end there.

His body was unceremoniously dumped into a grave on a nearby prairie, where it remained until the 1930s, when some local historians thought the outlaw deserved a better final resting place. So, according to local newspaper clippings from the time, thousands of spectators gathered to watch the exhumation, then followed the wagon to a new burial site in a community cemetery, where the body still rests. Today, the grave is denoted by a granite headstone rather than the wooden marker that once stood over his remains.

But Ketchum's troubles still weren't over.

In the 1950s he became the subject of a semi-fictional movie called *Black Jack Ketchum, Desperado*. It was mercilessly panned by the critics.

The entire story, including some rather gruesome photos of the actual execution, is on display in the Herzstein Memorial Museum.

For more information, visit www.herzsteinmuseum.org.

How to Succeed in Business
Clayton

A visit to the R. W. Isaacs Hardware Company (now Isaacs True Value Hardware) is a journey back to yesterday. The establishment still sells coal scuttles and washboards, its wooden floors still creak under the footsteps of the customers, and the same family has owned and operated it since 1890.

The current store sits on the original site in the heart of downtown, but it's not the original building. R. W. Isaacs, the founder, bought the first building in 1898. It was a combination *ferroteria* (iron store) and boardinghouse. When Isaacs decided to put up a new building on the same lot in 1908, he also wisely observed that business would suffer if he shut the store down during construction.

So he did what any smart businessman would do: He moved the original building. He moved it right onto an adjacent street, leaving room on one side so horses, buggies, and pedestrians could pass, and never missed a day of shopping. Then when the new building was complete, Isaacs tore down the old one and used the materials to build a new house. The replacement structure still maintains sentry duty at the corner of Main and First Streets.

A Flight Firstie

Clayton

Clayton has the distinction of being the first town in the United States to be authorized by the U.S. Postal Service as an airmail canceling center. But there was a bit of tomfoolery involved in earning the designation.

The year was 1914. The folks in Clayton were getting ready for the Union County Fair, held annually in the community. Airplanes and stunt pilots were big attractions at the time, so the committee in charge of entertainment came up with a plan to offer plane rides to the locals.

And then, in an apparent effort to take the venture to the next level, the planners evolved a scheme to have an airplane make flights from the fairgrounds to a temporary post office they set up near downtown, thereby creating airmail. The U.S. Postal Service issued a special stamp that was used to cancel letters and cards during

★ ★

Blown Away

The domed Union County Courthouse in Clayton was inspired by the architecture of the 1893 Worlds Fair in Chicago. Built in 1908, it replaced the original courthouse that was blown down by the only tornado ever to hit the city.

the promotion. It read: "First Aeroplane Postoffice, September 10, 1914."

The aviator and the plane were brought in from El Paso, Texas. The pilot arrived in one piece but the plane was shipped in three crates and had to be reassembled at the fair grounds. The local newspaper described it as "a machine that resembles a big grasshopper and sails through the air as light and graceful as a bird."

Hundreds took advantage of the offer to mail letters for two cents and postcards for a penny. When the plane took off, it circled the town, and dropped the mail pouch onto a vacant lot. Temporary postal workers retrieved the pouch, took it inside the temporary post office, canceled the stamps, and sent the mail on its way.

It was strictly a one-shot deal. Clayton still has an airport but the town never did become an airmail hub. However, it does have the only traffic signal in Union County, which is larger than Rhode Island and Delaware combined. The signal blinks red, yellow, and green at the intersection of Main and First Streets.

The Sign Bear(er)s
Eagle Nest

Nothing in Eagle Nest is very big. That includes the town itself. The population is slightly more than 300 and there are fewer than twenty

★ ★

buildings on the main drag. So the two big bears really stand out.

They're almost 10 feet tall, about the size of a Kodiak bear at full roar. They're harmless, however, because they're wood, not fur and fangs. They stand silently fulfilling their duties as sign-bearing bears along US 64 as it slices through the heart of the community.

Two bigger-than-life wooden bears serve as advertising icons in Eagle Nest.

Kevin Santana of Penrose, Colorado, carved the carnivorous couple, using a single log for each. And the sign they're holding is a promotion for Bear Mountain Estates . . . naturally.

Eagle Nest has a curious background because it was named after a lake instead of the other way around, as is the usual custom. The original town name was Therma in the early 1900s, when two developers spent eleven years building a dam across the mouth of Cimarron Canyon. They called the impounded body of water Eagle Nest Lake and stocked it with fish. That brought in the summer vacation crowd who heard news of the place back home. Then a whole bunch of letters addressed to Eagle Nest Lake instead of Therma began arriving, seeking information. Rather than trying to answer them and

★ ★

point out the mistake, the townspeople simply decided to make the change.

The community is in the heart of the Moreno Valley at 8,382 feet above sea level and surrounded by the Carson National Forest and the Sangre de Cristo Mountains. It's an easy drive from Taos (25 miles west on US 64) or Cimarron (20 miles east on the same road) in the summer but the area can get as much as 150 inches of snow in the winter.

Fortunately, that don't bother them bears none.

Tepees as Come-Ons
Eagle Nest

Two eras become as one at the Golden Eagle RV Park here, and at the Apache Ridge RV Park in Cimarron. Both places use tepees to grab the attention of those who pass by. The one here is made of cloth; Cimarron's is a more permanent structure made of gunite.

The irony is that the tepees are representations of housing from a long time ago, but they're now serving as eye-catchers for a new mode of living—those recreational vehicles that move from place to place at the direction of their owners.

Just like the tepees did.

RVers looking for a nice place to tie up and take on fresh water while getting rid of their used water will find the Golden Eagle park is at 540 West Therma Drive in Eagle Nest. Call (575) 377-6188 first to make sure there's room. The Apache Ridge Park is on Highway 21 in Cimarron.

Tepee aficionados and fans of inverted cones can also spot one in Chama directly across the street from the railroad station, and another one two miles west of Roswell at the Cactus Cave Gift Shop.

★ ★

Keeping the Prairie Safe

Elizabethtown

There's not much town left here. In fact, it's no longer listed on the map. But E-Town, as the locals call it, was at one time a boomtown created by miners who dug riches from the ground, spent the riches in local saloons and brothels, and then left once the good times ended. Now, only the Elizabethtown Museum pays tribute to those days.

Or, more romantically, maybe the people fled because of the dragon.

Well, probably not. The people were gone long before the dragon appeared.

He's sitting out there in the middle of a pasture. Typical dragon— green head, red eyes, and red nose, big jaws, mean looking. Only his

A steel dragon keeps a watchful eye out for knights in shining armor near Elizabethtown.

★ ★

head and tail are visible; the rest is hiding underground, waiting to
digest the remains of the unwary passerby who gets too close.

He's actually not much of a threat, however, because he's made of
steel culverts. John Mutz, a member of a prominent family of ranchers in the Moreno Valley, built him in the 1980s as a parade float for
a Fourth of July celebration in Red River. Once the festivities were
over, Mutz took the dragon back to his ranch and buried its midsec-
tion, thereby converting the beast into a bridge of sorts over a creek.

Knights in shining armor looking for a challenge can spot the creature on the west side of Highway 38 about 6 miles north of Eagle
Nest. There are no signs marking the dragon's lair so it takes keen
eyes to spot it. Those who do can pull off the road onto an approach
and walk 20 feet to a gate in the fence that surrounds the field
guarded by the fire-snorting reptile. But the land is posted so go no
farther. Unless, of course, you have no fear of either dragons or irate
farmers who might discourage trespassers with buckshot.

Tribute to a Really, REALLY Old Guy
Folsom

Here's the curious thing about the Folsom Man: None of his bones
have ever been found. Scientists have been working on the prehistoric man's existence ever since George McJunkin, a cowboy, discovered some skeleton parts in Wild Horse Arroyo back in the early
1920s. But the unearthed bones were those of a species of bison.

It wasn't until 1925 that scientists determined that the site was
one of the most important archaeological finds in the United States,
even though they found no human bones.

The reason for the Folsom Man designation is that the investigators also uncovered spear points among the bones and assumed that
since bison didn't have spear-making capabilities 25,000 years ago, the
points were made by man. So they scientifically deduced that the discovery of the points, coupled with evidence of nearby campsites, made
it a certainty that man had inhabited the area during the Ice Age.

★ ★

These were not, their reports said, ape men. They wore furs, made weapons, and were believed to have developed a language. Although chipped and chiseled from stone, some of the points on their weapons were as sharp as broken glass, and they varied in size, apparently depending upon the size of the prey being pursued.

Archaeologists had long believed the area was a fertile hunting ground for such finds because bones and other skeleton parts had been turning up for decades. The July 4, 1891, edition of the *Folsom Idea* reported the discovery of a mammoth's molar weighing about a pound and one-half. Since it was only a portion, the paper speculated that the entire tooth must have weighed between four and five pounds.

The research continues at the Folsom Man Archaeological Site, located 8 miles west of Folsom off Highway 72. And an inscription painted onto a large rock near the entrance proclaims: "Dedicated to the Folsom Man who long ago touched the sparks to the first campfire at this ancient site."

Dollars in the Antlers
Folsom

There's a small fortune hanging on the walls of the saloon at the Folsom Village Inn. The treasure contains thousands of pieces, and almost every piece is a $1 bill. They're everywhere—stapled to the walls; pinned to the ceiling, walls, and the bar itself; and impaled on the antlers of a stuffed deer head that looks down on the saloon.

This all started almost thirty years ago, when Mercedes and Richard Phillips opened the combination bar, restaurant, and lodging establishment. Mrs. Phillips pinned the first dollar the couple made in the venture to the wall, and patrons thought it was a novel idea so they started doing likewise.

Some of the bills are autographed, and some are foreign. And some big spenders have left their marks in the form of larger bills. But before you get ready to go rid the place of its riches, consider

★ ★

A Double Dose of History

Folsom, a small town in Union County, has ties to both prehistoric man and a candy bar. The town was named after Frances Ruth Folsom, President Grover Cleveland's bride and the mother of Ruth Cleveland, the couple's first child and the person for whom the Baby Ruth candy bar was named. And later, traces of a prehistoric humanoid were discovered north of the community and the archaeologists who uncovered the site named him the Folsom Man.

this: After a few years of serving as décor, the bills begin to deteriorate. "They just fall apart," said Tanya Garcia, a granddaughter of the founders and current owner of the place. She attributed it to cigarette smoke and kitchen residue. Despite that, nobody ever removes the bills for personal gain. "We let them hang there until they rot away," Garcia added. "We don't count them anymore, but at one time there were about 3,500 of them."

That's thirty-five hundred bucks. Or, in more recognizable terms, that's about fourteen hundred beers.

Got an extra dollar that's just itching to be hung someplace where everybody will see it and comment that they've never heard of you? The Folsom Village Inn is waiting on Highway 325. Investors and others can get more information by calling (575) 278-2478. And while you're waiting to make sure the thumb tack or piece of used bubble gum is firmly holding your contribution in place, you can order a Folsom burger, one of the house specialties.

What Population Explosion?

Harding County

This is an ideal place for those who love peace, quiet, and the absence of nosy neighbors who snoop over the back fence. Harding County covers 2,126 square miles. Of that total, 2,125 square miles are land; the other square mile is water. The largest city, population-wise, is Roy. About 300 people live there. The next most crowded town is Mills, with 50 residents.

The population of the entire county is less than 800. That means there are about 2.9 people per square mile. Only places like Antarctica and the Amazon rain forests have less density.

But what the county lacks in people, it makes up for in quiet and scenery. The town of Mosquero, for example, has a picturesque old courthouse that contains the only elevator in Harding County. And the City Bar is where locals tell authentic made-up stories about the wild times that used to happen in there.

Along the main street in Roy, the Floersheim Mercantile, built in 1897, and the 1930s Mesa Theater stand as reminders of a time gone by. The Sacred Heart of Jesus Church in Bueyeros was built in 1894 with a French design that includes a turquoise and copper steeple. The Church of the Immaculate Conception in Gallegos was constructed in 1914 using red sandstone blocks. The county also contains the Kiowa National Grasslands, the Canadian River Canyon, and numerous dinosaur tracks. •

And the nice thing about it is: Those who go there looking to enjoy the peace and quiet won't bump into a lot of camera-toting tourists asking where the nearest wine bar is located.

Voices in the Sky

Lamy

Today, there's nothing much unusual about this town except that it used to be called Galisteo Junction which isn't all that unusual

because name changes were commonplace in New Mexico back in the days before statehood. But on March 26, 1880, the gods who control curious and suspicious happenings selected the place for an uncommon occurrence.

According to local legend, UFO-ologists, and others who put trust in such reports, this is what happened:

On a quiet Friday night, three friends were walking down the main street when they heard voices that seemed to be coming from the sky. Naturally, they looked up—and saw an object "monstrous in size" approaching them. It was flying very low, and the occupants were laughing and shouting in an unfamiliar language. The men also heard strange music emitting from the craft, and they described it as "tinny-sounding." The thing hovering overhead, they said, was "fish-shaped" or "like a cigar with a tail," being driven by a large propeller.

As it passed over, one of the occupants tossed several items from the craft. One contained characters that the men thought were Asian. Then the machine ascended and took off at high speed. The men put the items on display at first but then sold most of them to a mysterious man of Asiatic origin who offered such a large sum that the offer couldn't be refused.

Then it got even weirder.

According to a story that appeared in the *Santa Fe Daily New Mexican*, a group of tourists stopped in the vicinity a couple days later. One of them was Chinese and he became very excited when he saw one of the remaining objects dropped from the flying craft because, he said, it was a note written by his fiancée. It was therefore assumed that the Chinese had succeeded in building an aircraft that made it all the way from China to Galisteo Junction.

Since it was never proved or disproved, the story still circulates around Lamy.

Lamy is about 7 miles south of Interstate 25, on the east side of Santa Fe, just off U.S. 285.

So Did They Send Her a Bill?

Las Vegas

Paula Angel had the dubious distinction of being the only woman ever hanged for murder in New Mexico. Her real name was Pablita Martin, and she was convicted of stabbing her lover in the back with a butcher knife in 1861 after he told her he was going home to his wife and children.

Justice was swift. Her trial was held five days later, and the presiding judge found her guilty and sentenced her to be hanged. Less than a month later, she was executed, but only after the first hanging didn't kill her. The second attempt was fatal and it was then revealed that the judge had also ordered her to pay the cost of all the legal action against her, including the cost of the hanging.

Along those same lines, a windmill was erected in the Las Vegas Plaza in 1876. For a brief time, it served as a vigilante gallows where suspected criminals were sent dangling to their dooms. Almost ironic, but somehow fitting, the town's original name was Nuestra Senora de los Dolores de Las Vegas (Our Lady of Sorrows of the Meadows).

Fortunately, things changed. The windmill, a sign of frontier justice, was replaced in 1880 by a bandstand surrounded by trees and a picket fence, and the square-block area was converted into the city's plaza.

The plaza is now shaded by old trees, and surrounded by buildings displaying a curious melange of architectural designs. For example, the Wesche-Dold Building is Greek Revival; the Veeder buildings combine a Moorish flavor with Tudor Revival; the E. Romero Hose and Fire Company building is Neo-Classical; and the Hedgecock building is Italianate style. They are among the more than 900 structures in Las Vegas listed on the National Register of Historic Places.

For more information on the city's past (and present), log onto www.lasvegasnm.com or call (800) 832-5947. The people there are very nice and they'll be exceptionally polite when they tell you that this isn't the Las Vegas where Wayne Newton performs.

★ ★

Keeping an Eye on the Wilderness
Maxwell

There's an eagle standing guard over the wild beauty of the Sangre de Cristo Mountains. It's a very large bird, probably 30 feet high, so obviously, it's not a real eagle. But it sure does look like one when viewed from the proper angle.

It's another of nature's whimsical creations, a natural rock formation located on a slope. And because it actually looks like what people say it looks like, it doesn't require squinting into the sunlight or using a whole lot of imagination to see the image.

Although it doesn't have an official name, the people in the area call it, logically, Eagle Rock. It's looking to the northwest and visible from I-25 on the west side of the freeway near exit 404 about 10 miles south of Springer. The area also contains rock formations known as Cathedral Rock and the Tooth of the Times. They're a bit harder to find, but ask anyone in Springer for directions.

A Slight Case of Overconfidence
Mills

Only a crumbling foundation marks the spot where Mills High School used to stand. The building was torn down in the 1960s when the town's population dipped so low that students were sent to other towns for their education.

But there was a time when everybody in Harding County and several surrounding counties knew about Mills High School and the basketball teams produced there.

For 16 years during the 1930s and 1940s, the Mills High School Bobcats were the crown princes of area basketball. Then 1940 came along and it was to be their best year ever. The team went through the entire regular season undefeated and was declared a sure bet to at least reach the state tournament.

And they probably would have, except for a severe case of cockiness.

★ ★

After beating a team from Farley by 50 points in the first round of the district tournament, the Bobcats were scheduled to play Springer in their next game. They had already defeated Springer by 20 points during the regular season, and they'd done it while using second-stringers for most of the game.

So the coach decided to give his starters the night off, and he sent them to the local pool hall so they could relax while the second-stringers got them to the next round. Bad mistake. Springer played one of its better games and led at the end of the third quarter. In near-panic, the coach rushed down to the pool hall to retrieve his regular starting lineup but by the time they got back to the gymnasium, the game had ended and the Bobcats' dreams of a perfect season were over. Springer won by a single point.

And now, just as the dream crumbled in 1940, the foundation of what used to be a school dissipates and fades away. And there probably won't be another chance to relive that time of near-glory because the current population of Mills is only 50.

One Tough Castle

Montezuma

The castle sits on top of a hill so it has a good view of the surrounding territory, which always makes sense when building a fortress. But this castle was never meant to be a castle. It was a hotel, and a mighty fine one.

The Atchison, Topeka and Santa Fe Railroad built the opulent first Montezuma Hotel in 1882 as an exclusive resort for passengers who might be interested in moving to, or investing in, the West. Located in Montezuma just outside Las Vegas, the site was ideal because it offered natural hot springs, good fishing, and ample room for hiking and sightseeing. But two years after the grand opening, the hotel's gas lines plugged up and caused a fire that destroyed the building.

Undaunted, the railroad built a new hotel on the same spot, but this time it was the first building in New Mexico wired for electricity. It also burned down.

And still undaunted, the railroad went right back to work and erected a third hotel on the spot, only this time it was named the Phoenix Hotel because

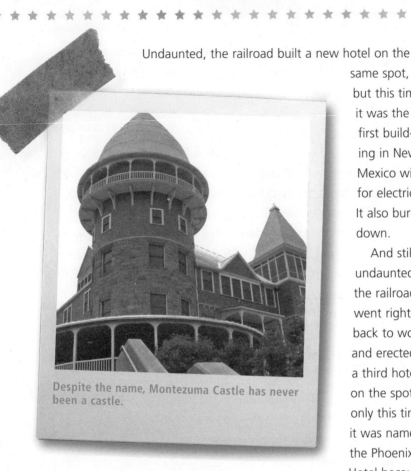

Despite the name, Montezuma Castle has never been a castle.

it, like the mythical bird, kept rising from the ashes. But the locals still called it the Montezuma, and its days were also numbered. Unable to compete with the newer and less swanky resorts, the hotel closed its doors in 1904. After sitting vacant for a number of years, the building was converted into a seminary and served in that capacity for thirty years.

The Armand Hammer Foundation bought the property in 1981 and established the American campus of the United World College on the grounds. But the castle remained closed because it needed extensive repairs, so the college used other buildings as classrooms and dormitories. Then in 1997, the castle/hotel was named one of eleven on a list of America's 11 Most Endangered Historic Places and the following year, a White House council identified it as one of America's treasures. All that attention led to fund-raising, followed by renovation. Now the castle has come full circle. Since 2002 it has served as living space for students and visitors.

And it is once again known as Montezuma Castle.

To get to the college campus and the castle, take exit 343 off I-25. Go ½ mile and turn left onto New Mexico Avenue. Go 1.9 miles to the first traffic light, where you will turn left again onto Hot Springs Boulevard and continue a little over 4 miles, turning right when you see Montezuma's Castle. For more information, go to www.uwc-usa .org/about/montezumacastle.htm or call (505) 454-5221.

Montezuma is on Highway 65 about 11 miles northeast of Las Vegas.

One Big Star for Wishing Upon

Moriarty

The thing that looks like a star on top of El Comedar de Anayas is an attention-grabber not only because of its size (about 16 feet from point to point) but also because it's blue.

And red and yellow.

And gold.

With orange and green parts.

It looks more like a piñata or a Christmas tree ornament than a star, but it was put up there by the Anayas family and they called it a star. They own the restaurant so they can call it anything they want. Actually, it's neither a piñata nor a star. It's a roto-sphere, one of several examples of spiky signage that encourage people to stop at restaurants, motels, and shopping malls all across the nation. They all resemble Sputnik, the space machine shot into the atmosphere by the Russians in 1957.

This one has 16 points and was hoisted up to the roof in the 1990s as part of a remodeling project after a fire destroyed much of

★ ★

the building. Each spike is lined with neon tubing and they all light up at night, casting a glow that can be seen all over Moriarty and clear out to Interstate 40 north of town.

At one time, it also revolved. The aluminum spikes are mounted on a large ball composed of two counter-rotating hemispheres that are driven by a Model A differential. But the mechanism broke down in 2006 and hasn't been fixed. It still lights up at night, however.

The restaurant, owned by the family through four generations, was once a popular stop for Route 66 travelers who passed directly in front of the establishment. It has also been a gathering place for politicians and celebrities whose photographs hang on the walls.

Got a big wish that needs a star, or a tummy that needs a burrito? The El Comedar is at 1005 Route 66 in the heart of Moriarty. Or call (505) 832-4442, but don't expect Jiminy Cricket to answer the phone.

Washing Machine Sculpture
Mountainair

Gordon McMath's sense of humor and his wife's persistent insistence are the main reasons he became an artist. After he retired from a lengthy career as a dry land bean farmer, McMath began collecting things: small things, medium-sized things, and even some big things.

Things like old washing machines, car parts, water heaters, gadgets, gizmos and whatchamacallits. Once collected, the items just sat there, waiting to be reborn in different forms or otherwise put to new use. But in the meantime, they were cluttering up his house, garage, and yard.

Until his wife Biddie took action.

"I kept on fussin' at him to do something with all the junk," she says with a chuckle. And so, in the early 1990s, McMath became a sculptor. He began creating statuary, using not marble or clay or bronze, but the inner workings of old washers and automobiles to make half-size figures of people and other creatures. The end results are cowboys wearing hats made of tractor seats, pioneer women clad in tin bonnets, and animals created from old springs.

Many of his works stand in the front yard, waving at the folks who pass by. Others have taken up residency in other homes because McMath sells one "ever now and then." His work has also been featured in a *Smithsonian Magazine* article about art in New Mexico.

McMath calls it junk art and figures he'll keep on making it until his supplies run out, which won't be very soon because his garage is filled with cogs, gears, coils, magnetos and other sculpting materials.

Art critics and appliance repairmen will find his work at the corner of Ripley and Third Street, a couple blocks south of U.S. 60 as it bisects the town.

Is That a Tibetan Monk or a Sweet Potato?
Questa

Stuart Wilde's collection isn't very big in quantity but makes up for it in size. He collects llamas. And as a result, he also knows how to pronounce "llama."

Wilde doesn't actually collect the animals in the sense that he goes to thrift stores and garage sales looking for them. They sort of come to him. He started in 1991 by purchasing a pair of llamas on a time payment plan. "A hundred dollars down and a hundred a month," he says. Then he acquired others from people who bought them as pets and couldn't handle them, or from people getting out of the llama-raising business.

Now he has fourteen of the furry creatures and he uses most of them in his business, known as Wild Earth Llama Adventures. They serve as pack llamas, carrying supplies for the paying customers on treks through pine forests and alpine meadows in the Sangre de Cristo Mountains and the Rio Grande Gorge.

Trek guides have extensive knowledge of the area flora, fauna, ecology, history, which plants are edible, and how to survive in the wilderness if your llama suddenly decides to hitchhike back to the Andes Mountains in Peru where their ancestors came from. The guides assure trekkers that it won't happen, but do point out that the ancient Inca tribes depended on llamas and that these are descendants of the creatures that carried supplies to the fabled Machu Picchu. This, of course, gives the trekker a sense of being an integral part of history in a generational remote sort of way.

And about the pronunciation of "llama," Wilde prefers "yama" because, he says, it honors the language of their Spanish-speaking homelands in South America where two consecutive *l*'s translate into *y*. But he doesn't correct those who say "lama," because that's the anglicized version as it appears in the dictionary. Anyway, linguists and hikers alike can get more information by logging onto www.LlamaAdventures.com or calling (800) 758-LAMA (5262).

Living Around in the Round
Questa

There wasn't enough room for his family and friends in the caboose, so Duane Huseman bought two big steel ball-shaped tanks, and now everybody can come up to his place and have themselves, well, a ball!

Huseman, who lives in Nazareth, Texas, moved a caboose to his property in the Sangre de Cristo Mountains in 1983 in lieu of building a cabin. It worked fine for his family, but he had no room for friends. So one day while driving near Amarillo, Texas, he spotted the two huge tanks. He inquired, discovered they were pressure cookers from a paper mill in Virginia, and bought them because he figured that with some modifications, they'd make a nice guesthouse.

After an extended period of cutting and welding, he moved the tanks up to the mountains, where he insulated them, plastered the interior, installed doors and windows, built a passageway between them, and mounted them on steel cylinders. One tank contains

★ ★

Photo: Craig Kerkman.

Old pressure cookers have been converted
into a cabin in the woods.

the bedroom and bathroom; the other holds the kitchen and living
quarters.

There's plenty of room inside because the tanks are 15 feet in
diameter and it's 10 feet from floor to ceiling. And they're pretty
sturdy. The steel is 1½ inches thick and each tank weighs 40,000
pounds. Huseman started working on the project in 1999 and still
has some minor details to complete. "Little did I know how much
work it was going to be," he said. "Without my family and friends
from Nazareth and Amarillo, it would never have happened."

The cabin in the round is located in the woods east of Questa but
don't try to get there without detailed directions and, since Huseman
would prefer it if a lot of snoopy people didn't start showing up at
his place, he doesn't give out detailed directions.

How'd You Get That Name?
Questa

A nice little town of about 2,000 residents, Questa is nestled at the foot of the Sangre de Cristo mountain range, but its current name bears only a slight resemblance to what it was originally called.

The area was first settled in 1829 and the town was officially founded in 1842, when it was named San Antonio Del Rio Colorado (St. Anthony of the Red River) after its patron saint. But it was later changed by an American postmaster who renamed it "Cuesta," the Spanish word for "slope" because the town sits on a mountainside. But the postmaster didn't know how to spell "Cuesta" so he wrote "Questa."

And, to make it a bit more confusing, it's still pronounced "kwesta" like the postmaster intended instead of "kaysta," which would be the proper was to say it in Spanish.

Regardless of how it's pronounced, Questa has a couple of interesting curiosities. One is the oldest surviving building in town, San Antonio de Padua Catholic Church, which was constructed in 1841. The church resembles a fortress, similar to the one erected to keep out raiding Utes and Apaches. It probably offered protection from both marauders and grizzly bears and should have served well because its adobe walls are 5 feet thick.

Questa, 7,655 feet above sea level, is tucked between the Rio Grande and the Sangre de Cristo Mountains about 21 miles north of Taos on Highway 522.

My, What Big Paws You Have!
Raton

The road leading to Raton High School would look like any other strip of pavement that winds through a residential area up to an institution of learning except for the paw prints in one traffic lane. They're big and they're yellow, and they go for a couple of miles up the street, heading directly toward the school.

The reason for their existence is that the school's athletic teams are nicknamed the Tigers. The paw prints are placed on the streets by the Tiger Paws, a team support group that applies a new coat of paint to the markings every fall before football season begins.

"They're an example of school spirit, and they make it easy to find the school because you just follow the paws," according to Mike Sparaco, the school principal. "They're also meant to intimidate other teams who come here to play the Tigers."

The paw prints start on Tiger Drive, an extension of Clayton Road where it intersects with South Second Street. They lead directly west, to the high school.

Ironically, "raton" is Spanish for "mouse" and the town got its name because the original settlers mistook prairie dogs for rats. They're gone now, at least most of them. The giant paw prints may or may not have had something to do with it.

To see the tiger prints, take exit 451 off I-25 and go west on Clayton Road. Go straight through the intersection with US 64/I-25 Business Loop, onto Tiger Drive. Follow Tiger Drive to the high school.

When a Name Change Was Necessary
Raton

The International Bank is housed in a wonderful old three-story brick structure that was built in 1929 as a hotel. The building was decorated at the roofline with swastikas, an Indian symbol of good luck, and became a Raton landmark known, quite naturally, as the Swastika Hotel. But that all changed in the 1940s.

When Adolph Hitler and the Nazis grabbed power in Germany prior to World War II, they adopted the swastika as their party symbol. So when the United States entered the war, the lodging establishment quickly changed its name from the Swastika Hotel to the Yucca Hotel.

The swastikas still adorn the top of the building, but today, only the old-timers remember when they weren't a welcome sight.

★ ★

The Beers Are Talking Back!

In an effort to keep drunks off the road by lecturing them, the New Mexico Department of Transportation paid $21 each for 500 talking urinal deodorizer-cake holders and installed them in men's restrooms across the state.

The placement is logical because the urinal is frequently the last place an overimbiber will stop at before hitting the road. So when a man steps up, the motion-sensitive plastic device activates and the voice of a woman says, "Hey, big guy. Having a few drinks? Think you had one too many? Then it's time to call a cab or call a sober friend for a ride home."

And then, after a brief pause, the message ends with "Remember, your future is in your hand."

There have been no studies on whether or not the devices work, but they're definitely attention getters. And shortly after they were installed in a bar in Rio Rancho, three of them were stolen. NMDOT officials are still waiting for them to show up on eBay.

To see the bank, from I-25 take either exit 450 or 454, onto the Business Loop and follow it through town. The building will be on the corner of South Second Street and Cook Avenue. Although the old Swastika Hotel has the most interesting story, a couple of other Raton buildings are worth mentioning because of some quirks and curiosities. One of them is the Abourezk Building, erected in 1906. Its facade is adorned with garlands and two female figureheads. It's on the west side of First Street, between Cook and Park Avenues.

The Coors Brewing Company built the Coors Building at a local warehouse in 1906. The building shares a common wall with the Haven Hotel which agreed to serve only Coors beer forever in return for the arrangement. That deal ended when the brewers left town. The building now houses the Raton Museum, also located on First Street between Cook and Rio Grande avenues.

Driving with Drumsticks
Red River

While most people stay at home on Thanksgiving enjoying roasted turkey and all the stuff that goes with it, there are others who spend the day utilizing the bird in a completely different fashion:

They ride frozen turkeys down a ski slope.

One of the winter events at the Red River Ski Area is the annual Turkey Toboggan, in which competitors careen down the snow-covered hills while seated on an unthawed turkey. It's been going on for about a decade, and up to forty bird racers compete every Thanksgiving. Usually, each contestant gets a couple of slides, which are timed to determine the winner. But sometimes the field gets so big that the racers get only one run down the beginners' slope.

Since frozen turkeys are rather difficult to steer, even when using the drumsticks as directional devices, spinouts and runaway carcasses are commonplace. The ski lodge furnishes the turkeys, which is probably a big relief to Thanksgiving cooks who would rather prepare a fresh bird than one that's been sat on.

For those who prefer something a little easier on the backside, the ski resort also offers cross-country skiing, Saturday night torchlight parades, and snowmobile rides to the top of 11,249-foot Greenie Peak. During the summer, when jockeying frozen turkeys and riding flat slats down a mountain lose their popularity, Red River features drives along the Enchanted Circle Scenic Byway, rides on the ski lifts, arts and crafts fairs, wine festivals, chile cook-offs, and crosstown excursions on the trolley.

★ ★

Daredevils looking for something more exciting than cranberry sauce and football games on Thanksgiving can get more information by logging on to www.redriverskiarea.com or by calling the lodge at (575) 754-2223.

The Art of the Discard
Ribera

Nicasio "Nick" Romero creates sculpture out of, well, just about anything. His materials include 8-by-8 timbers, beer bottles, logs, car parts, dirt, cement, and adobe. One of his more spectacular creations is Millennium, an 8-foot adobe tower hidden in the trees near his studio. Another is a woodpile. Not an ordinary woodpile, but one with the pieces swirled to form an igloo-like structure. And down near a small creek that flows through his property is the skeleton of a horse, made of scrap tin.

Artist Nick Romero uses just about anything to create his sculptures near Ribera.

They, and many more of equal interest, are on display at the El Ancon Outdoor Sculpture Show, an array of nontraditional sculpture that occupies space on both sides of the dirt road that wanders by his studio. On the north side Romero

★ ★

has created a kiva, a watchtower, and several *hornos* (ovens) that are guarded by a welded steel rhinoceros. But the really good stuff is across the road.

He has converted old timbers into cricket players who swing huge bats through the mountain air. He has created a band of musicians from old machine parts, and abstract forms and shapes from twigs and pieces of cloth. He has also twisted supple tree branches into large hanging baskets.

To get to Ribera, take exit 323 on I-25 and go south on Highway 3. The art show is located about a mile northwest of town. Take the dirt road just north of the railroad tracks and head west.

Some Claims to Fame

Roy

Even though it has a population of about only 300, Roy is the largest community in Harding County. The town used to be larger, back when it was a major distribution point for wheat, beans, dairy products, and cattle before the Dust Bowl ended its heyday as an agricultural hub in the 1920s.

Today, one of Roy's major claims to fame is that Bob Wills once cut hair in a local barbershop. And that's important because Wills also wrote a song he titled "Spanish Two Step" while he lived here. He later changed it to "San Antonio Rose," which became a major hit after he moved on to form Bob Wills and His Texas Playboys, one of the leading Western bands in the 1940s. In 1945 Wills reportedly was earning $350,000 per year and his group was outdrawing the bands led by Tommy Dorsey and Benny Goodman. He also appeared in several movies and his records were top sellers. He died in 1976 at age 70.

There are no museums, plaques, or other memorials that immortalize Wills's skills with either a fiddle or a pair of clippers, but the old-timers still talk about his two-year stay here, and a couple of area bands have resurrected his music.

★ ★

Roy was also home to another nationally known personality. Tommy McDonald, an All-American running back on the University of Oklahoma's national championship team and All-Pro wide receiver with the Philadelphia Eagles, started playing football at Roy High School. He's now in pro football's Hall of Fame in Canton, Ohio.

Was D.H. Ditched?
San Cristobal

During his lifetime English novelist D. H. Lawrence was a center of controversy because of his writing. And today, almost eight decades after his death, he's still involved in controversy, but now it's about his ashes.

There's agreement about what happened up to a point: Lawrence died in 1930 and was buried in Vence, France, but his remains were exhumed and cremated in 1935. From there on, it gets confusing.

One version says that his widow, Frieda, gave the ashes to her lover, Angelo Ravagli, with instructions to take them to the Kiowa Ranch near San Cristobal, where the Lawrences had lived for a couple of years. That version says Ravagli fulfilled his mission and spread the ashes over the property.

However, an offshoot of that scenario has Ravagli admitting after several years (and several shots of bourbon) that he dumped the ashes in France to avoid the expense and trouble of transporting them across the ocean. He then sent the empty container to New York, where he picked it up and filled it with locally procured ashes, which he took to the ranch and tossed to the winds. Another version says Ravagli got the substitute ashes to the ranch and mixed them in with some concrete being poured as a slab.

But did that actually happen?

Not according to the other stories. In them Ravagli (a) took the ashes to the ranch and placed them and the urn on the mantel in the ranch house; (b) took the ashes to the ranch and waited for Frieda to arrive and they both spread the remains over the ranch; or (c) took the ashes to the ranch and, following Frieda's orders, mixed them with the mortar used to erect a shrine to Lawrence's memory.

And in the Way Out There Department, one theory suggests that the ashes were eaten by Witter Bryner, an American author who often associated with Lawrence.

Regardless of which tale, if any, is true, Frieda deeded the ranch to the University of New Mexico before her death and it's now open to the public. Watch for the signs on the east side of Highway 522 about 10 miles north of Taos; turn east on Forest Road 493 for 1 mile, south on Old Highway 3 for ½ mile, and then east on Camino Del Medio for 1½ miles.

The Mysterious Stairs

Santa Fe

For more than a century, the staircase in the Loretto Chapel was considered a miracle, or at least, a work of unexplainable carpentry.

The legend goes back to about 1873, when the Sisters of Loretto had a chapel built next to their school for girls. But the architect died before completing the plans and left no design for a staircase to get from the main floor to the choir loft. The nuns appealed to local craftsmen but received no help, other than suggestions that they use a ladder. So, according to the oft-told story, for nine days they prayed to St. Joseph, the carpenter. On the ninth day, according to the legend, a man showed up with a donkey and a toolbox and said he could handle the project.

He built a circular staircase that took up little room and gave the nuns access to the loft, and he did it without using glue or nails. Then, the legend goes, he disappeared without asking for either payment or thanks, and the rumors started that it was St. Joseph himself who had come to the rescue. Adding more mystery to the story was the theory that the wood used was impossible to find in the area.

As the legend grew, so did the crowds who came to see the miraculous staircase. But in the 1990s skeptics started looking closely at

★ ★

the work and then set about debunking the story. Their investigations concluded that the stairs were built by a Frenchman, Francois-Jean Rocha, and they produced records that indicate he bought the wood from a local lumberyard. Also, the doubters claim, Rocha's obituary in the *Santa Fe New Mexican* in 1895 said he was the builder.

Despite that, the legend persists. And regardless of whether it's fact or fiction, the staircase itself is a remarkable piece of woodworking. The chapel is now owned by the adjacent Inn at Loretto. The public can still view the staircase but there's an entry fee, payable at the front desk of the hotel.

Off I-25 take exit 282 (282B if you are coming from the east), and go north on Highway 14/Saint Francis Drive, following it to Highway 589. Go east on 589, and then turn north where that road meets Old Santa Fe Trail. The chapel is located at 207 Old Santa Fe Trail. For more information, log on to www.lorettochapel.com or call (505) 982-0092.

A Double-Horned Bunny
Santa Fe

The world's largest jackalope sits in Douglas, Wyoming. It's made of fiberglass and guards the front entrance of the local fair grounds. Douglas is a natural location for this monument because the American jackalope's heritage can be directly traced there. Also, Wyoming trademarked the name in 1965 and even issues hunting licenses for the elusive creature.

But the world's largest *blue* jackalope stands silent watch in front of Jackalope, one in the chain of import/export/antique stores here.

The critter is made of wood and spent most of its life hidden away in one of the store's back lots. But then it was resurrected, given a paint job, and placed in front of the establishment in the hope that it would draw customers, not scare them away. Mexican artist Alejandrino Fuentes gave the hybrid bunny its new look, accenting the basic blue with reds and whites.

The legend of horned rabbits probably started in Europe in the 1500s and then moved across the Atlantic. In the 1930s Douglas taxidermist Doug Herrick conjured up the species by mounting the horns of a small antelope on a jackrabbit's head. The creature not only earned Herrick quite a bit of money but also took on a life of its own. Jackalopes are common inhabitants of gift shops and curio stores, and there are all sorts of jackalope rumors floating around, like the one that says it has developed vocal cords and often sings at night on the open prairie.

The big one's not for sale, but believers and nonbelievers alike can purchase jackalopes of all shapes and sizes at the store. There's even one that has a jackalope head mounted on the body of a chicken. It may, or may not, be the real thing. The

A large blue jackalope attracts customers to a Santa Fe commercial enterprise.

phone number is (505) 867-9813 but those who call shouldn't expect a jackalope to answer because it's beneath the creature's dignity to perform such menial tasks. After all, they are international icons.

Take exit 278 (278B if you are coming from the east) on I-25 and go north on Highway 14/Cerrillos Road. The store is located at 2820 Cerrillos Road. For more information, visit www.jackalope.com/location_santafe.html or call (505) 471-8539.

★ ★

Didn't They Know the Way to Santa Fe?
Santa Fe

The Atchison, Topeka and Santa Fe Railway were partially named after this city. And in the 1940s, composers Harry Warren and Johnny Mercer wrote "On the Atchison, Topeka and the Santa Fe" for *The Harvey Girls,* a movie starring Judy Garland.

But there's something misleading about these historical designations. The Atchison, Topeka and Santa Fe Railway never got to Santa Fe. At least, not directly.

The railroad had crossed into New Mexico by 1878 and was scheduled to reach Santa Fe. But the city refused to pay for the costs involved so the AT&SF opted for an 18-mile spur that ran from Santa Fe to Lamy, a smaller community to the south.

Santa Fe had relied on the Santa Fe Trail to bring in trade and commerce and hoped that the railroad would bring the same good fortune, but once the railroad's main line bypassed the city, the revenue stream shifted to Las Vegas and Albuquerque. In an effort to reverse the situation, the railroad began offering free transportation to artists who, hopefully, would promote travel to the then-remote area through their paintings. But that effort backfired when most of the artists were drawn to Taos instead of Santa Fe. Despite that, Santa Fe survived, quite well, in fact, and is now the state capital.

Open Air Arias
Santa Fe

The Santa Fe Opera has a certain airiness about it because the artists and musicians are literally singing outdoors. The opera house has a unique roof system and one solid wall, but the other three sides are open to the elements. This allows patrons a chance to watch a sunset and listen to the breezes while they're enjoying *La Bohéme* and *Madama Butterfly.*

✳ ✳

The current building was completed in 1998 as a replacement for two earlier theaters erected on the same 199 acres that years ago were the site of a guest ranch. The first venue was totally open air and was placed there after the company's founder and an architect checked the acoustics by firing a series of rifle shots into the air to determine how well the sound would carry. The second theater had a sort of half roof but the sides of the structure were open so the performers and audience were still exposed to thunderstorms, rain, and high winds.

The new opera house, finished and opened in 1998, features a complete roof structure that resembles sails, and large baffles that hold down the wind noise. But it has no fly system that would allow scenery to be lowered from the ceiling so the backdrops are brought up from underneath the stage on a huge elevator. As a result, audiences occasionally get to enjoy an ever-changing background of sunsets and thunderstorms during productions that don't use backdrops.

Also, there's no proscenium arch, which means no curtains and no place to project subtitles. However, in a classic example of Santa Fe adaptability, the opera utilizes a system that shows subtitles on the backs of seats, and they can be translated into eight different languages.

Since it opened, the house has been the scene of more than 40 American premieres and nine new operas commissioned by the company.

Follow US 285 north out of downtown to exit 168. Turn left at the end of the exit ramp, and then right onto the frontage road (Opera Drive). Go 1.4 miles to the opera. For more information on how to hear the high notes on a high mesa, log on to www.santafeopera.org or call (800) 280-4654.

Burning Their Cares Away
Santa Fe

Every year around the first week of September, Santa Feans have an opportunity to watch their troubles go up in smoke, and they do this

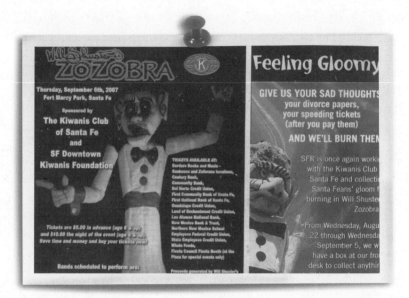

Newspaper ads herald the annual immolation of Zozobra in Santa Fe.

with considerable enthusiasm. As part of the annual Fiesta de Santa Fe, a huge marionette named Zozobra gets burned at the stake while thousands of onlookers cheer. It's because Zozobra is also known as Old Man Gloom, and his body is allegedly stuffed with all the trials, tribulations, woes, and travails of the previous year.

The fiesta has been held every year since 1712 to commemorate the retaking of the city from the Pueblo Indians. But Zozobra didn't become part of the celebration until 1924, when artist Will Shuster built one and invited some friends to his home where they theoretically disposed of their troubles by turning them into ashes. Shuster based his creation on a Yaqui Indian custom of burning an effigy of Judas during Holy Week. The creator turned all rights to Zozobra over to the local Kiwanis Club in 1964, and the organization has not only continued the tradition, but also used it to earn more than $300,000 for scholarships.

Cooking with Earth

There was a time when the only *hornos* in New Mexico were found in the pueblos. Not anymore. Today, the beehive-shaped earthen ovens are popping up in cities and towns all over the state. And their new popularity is helping clear up some common misconceptions about their origins.

For years most believed they were created by the Pueblo Indians who originally settled here. But hornos probably originated in Egypt more than 3,000 years ago. They came to New Mexico with the Spanish, who may have copied the idea from their African neighbors and then brought them along while exploring New Mexico in the 1500s. Regardless of how they got here, hornos are now common in southwestern décor.

But they're not just for show. Most are used for baking because, according to some veteran bakers, bread and other things taste better when cooked in one. The ovens are commonly made of adobe brick covered with either adobe or cement plaster. They range from small family units to the large size that can bake up to sixty loaves at a time.

The baking process is simple: Light a big fire inside the horno using a hot-burning wood like cedar or juniper. Let the fire burn for several hours to heat up the stones and earth. When the fire has burned down to coals, scrape them out because the oven will hold heat up to 500 degrees for several hours. Insert the food and wait.

Ready to build one? Go find a copy of *Build Your Own Earth Oven* by Kiko Denzer and Hannah Field.

Because Zozobra is destroyed every year, a new one has to be made the next year. The figure stands about 50 feet tall and is made of precut wooden strips covered with chicken wire and muslin and then painted. The body is stuffed with shredded paper, usually things like police reports, divorce papers, and paid-off mortgages. The creation process takes up to three weeks and involves an estimated 3,500 volunteer hours.

And then, in front of as many as 40,000 onlookers, it begins waving its arms and uttering ferocious growls as the flames surround it, destroying all the cares and troubles of the past.

If you wish to go, check out www.zozobra.com. Even last-minute attendees are invited to include their "troubles." A gloom box is placed near the band stage at the lost and found, and all articles are added right before Zozobra is burned at dusk.

The festivities begin at dusk in Fort Marcy Park and require admission tickets. There's no parking near the site, but park and ride options are available at local malls and bus terminals. The event has also spawned a line of merchandise that goes on sale during the fiesta. Items include T-shirts, stickers, shot glasses, temporary tattoos, pins, earrings, ball caps, beanies, and DVDs. They're available at a Zozobra booth on the downtown plaza in the days before and after the immolation.

Amateur pyromaniacs who need more information can find it by calling the Zozobra hotline, (505) 660-1965, or logging on to www .zozobra.com.

Washing Time Away
Santa Rosa

The history of Santa Rosa is carved in stone but you don't need a hieroglyphics expert to decipher it. Even better, you can cool off while studying the town's origins because they're depicted on a fountain.

It's 12 feet tall and made of three cast stone blocks stacked atop each other. The blocks diminish in size as they go up, so the bottom piece is about 10 feet square while the top one measures about 4 feet by 4 feet. Each is illustrated with symbols that relate to the city and Guadalupe County. They include reproductions of petroglyphs, rivers, lakes, early railroad workers, old cars, a bridge, churches, Spanish explorers, and farming and ranching scenes.

The fountain sits as the centerpiece of the Courthouse Plaza, a city streetscape project that was finished in 2008. The plaza is located on the corner of Fourth Street and Historic Route 66, right in the heart of downtown.

Santa Rosa is on Interstate 40 about 110 miles east of Albuquerque.

Scuba Diving in the Desert
Santa Rosa

The countryside surrounding Santa Rosa is so semiarid it's almost a desert. It's suitable for ranching and Sunday drives in an ATV, but at first glance, the area would have nothing that could possibly appeal to a diver. But it does, and the place has become a mecca for those who put on wet suits and inhale the contents of a scuba tank.

The primary destination is a large pond a few blocks from downtown called the Blue Hole, an 80-foot-deep geological phenomenon shaped like a bell A. It's always full of water, and the Blue Hole's temperature is a constant 62 degrees. The water is remarkably clear, and there's even a training platform about a third of the way to the bottom. It's on Blue Hole Road, a half-mile south of Guadalupe County Hospital.

But don't just drive up and jump in. Before immersing themselves, divers need the proper certification papers in order to get a permit that allows them to dunk themselves. The permits are available at the Visitor Information Center downtown, online, or at the dive center at the pool, which also rents equipment.

Another "must see" for the wet suit is the twin-engine plane that sank in 55 feet of water at nearby Perk Lake, which is 2 miles southeast of Santa Rosa on Highway 91. For more information or to print a

★ ★

permit to dive, visit www.santarosanm.org or call the Visitor Information Center at (507) 472-3763.

A House of the Big
Springer

The Santa Fe Trail Interpretive Center and Museum goes for big things in a big way. At least, a couple of its exhibits give that impression.

One of the first things visitors see when approaching the museum is a 10-foot-tall statue of an early settler. It's a wood carving of a man wearing a sombrero, holding a shotgun, and staring at the Ten Commandments painted on a large stone across the walkway. The carving was done by D. D. White in 1996.

A 10-foot woodcarving guards the entry to a Springer museum.

The museum, housed in the old Colfax County Court House, was built in 1882. Inside, one of the star attractions is a huge brown wingtip shoe that once belonged to Robert Wadlow. At 8 feet, 11 inches, he was the world's tallest man. And even today, almost seventy years after his death, no human has surpassed that height. The closest anyone has come is Leonid Stadnik, a Ukrainian who stands 8 feet, 5 inches tall.

The shoe is a size 37. It looks like something a gardener might use as a planter. Not even today's gigantic professional basketball players wear shoes that big. Initially, Wadlow had to pay about $100 per pair (a staggering sum because this was back in the Great Depression of the 1930s). But then he went to work for the International Shoe Company, which provided him with free footwear. While traveling around the country as a representative of the company, Wadlow often left his shoes with merchants so they could display them in their stores. That's probably how one got all the way to Springer from his hometown of Alton, Illinois. Wadlow died in 1940 at the age of 22.

Also on display, but not quite as interesting as a big shoe and a big settler, is New Mexico's first (and only) electric chair. It's real, but the frightened executionee sitting in it is a mannequin.

To reach the museum at 514 Maxwell Avenue take either exit 412 or 414 off I-25 and head into town on U.S. Highway 85, which turns into Maxwell Avenue. The museum is located on the east side of the street between Fifth and Sixth. For more information about the Santa Fe Trail in general or the museum in particular, visit www.santa fetrailnm.org or call the museum at (575) 483-5554.

Keeping an Eye on The Food

Taos

Eating a meal in the Kiva Coffee Shop can be a bit unnerving if you feel uncomfortable when there's somebody or something watching each spoonful you launch stomachward.

The dining spot, located in the Best Western Kachina Lodge, was built by Edwin Lineberry, who patterned it after the kivas found in many of the Native American pueblos and villages in New Mexico and Arizona. So it's round, and the ceiling is held up by a series of *vigas* (log poles) that extend like spokes from a center column to the edges.

It's that center column that catches the eye, in a very real sense. It's a totem pole, designed and carved by artist Duane Van-Vechten, Lineberry's wife. It's very big and it sits in the middle of a circular counter and the eyes look right down into your bacon and eggs. Since the eyes are in proportion to the totem, they're also

★ ★

A Very Litter-ary Bird

Although they're not the official state birds, turkey vultures are New Mexico icons because (a) they're so magnificently ugly and (b) they assist in the task of keeping the landscape clean with their dining habits. They eat dead things. And their bald, red heads help them in the task because baldness eliminates such problems as carrion getting caught in the face feathers, which could lead to insect infestations around the beak.

In their role as scavengers, the vultures recycle dead things like roadkill into the food chain while cleaning up the environment. All this makes their Latin name even more fitting. It's *cathartes,* which means "purifier."

very big, so they create an impression that you'd better watch your manners because there's something monster-sized keeping an eye on you.

The lodge and coffee shop, at 413 Paseo del Pueblo Norte, can be reached by following US 64 through town. The lodge is on the east side of the road between Brook Street and Montecito Lane. For reservations or more information, telephone (575) 758-2275.

Low-Budget Park

Taos

The Holy Trinity Park is a vacant lot in the heart of downtown Taos on what would seem to be a piece of prime real estate. Instead, it's covered with homemade signs and a confusing theme that makes references to religion, war, peace, philosophy, and doing good things.

The park is a labor of love by R. E. Boge, a self-described "feeble amateur artist." According to a written statement posted on a tree, the idea came about thusly: "Several years ago, the Holy Spirit and I picked up a truck load of garbage, and filled in some very deep ruts left by high rise pickups. Everything was done by the Holy Spirit and yours truly." The "everything" referred to consists of pictures clipped from magazines, some religious icons, little altars, and one series of signs that read, "I ain't what I should be. I ain't what I oughta be. But thank God, I ain't what I was."

Repeated inquiries in the area about the park and the whereabouts of the artist drew blank stares, sighs, and snorts. But it's a quiet place amid the hustle of the tourist trade that sustains Taos. Peace seekers will find it on Paseo del Pueblo Norte, right in the heart of downtown.

The Earth Is Cracking!
Taos

The landscape northwest of Taos is so flat that it's possible to see for miles in any direction. But then, all at once and with very little warning, the earth makes a sudden turn.

Straight down.

It's the Rio Grande Gorge, a gulch that plunges more than 200 yards down to the river below and promises to put some pretty bad hurt on anyone or anything that falls in. Fortunately, there's a bridge across the gap and the bridge is lined with steel side rails so chances of accidentally driving off the edge are relatively remote, if not completely impossible.

The Rio Grande Gorge Bridge is the third highest cantilevered bridge in the United States, towering 650 feet above the river. It is surpassed in height only by the Royal Gorge Bridge (1,053 feet) over

★ ★

the Arkansas River in Colorado and the New River Bridge (876 feet) over the New River in West Virginia.

It was dedicated on Sept. 10, 1965, and has been named the "most beautiful steel bridge" in the long span category by the American Institute of Steel Construction. Also, it has appeared in such movies as *Natural Born Killers, She's Having A Baby,* and the immortal *Twins,* which featured Danny DiVito and Arnold Schwarzenegger as twin brothers.

Those who wouldn't get uptight about looking straight down from the top of a sixty-five-story skyscraper will find good viewing areas on both sides of the bridge's 600-foot main center span. There are ample parking spaces and vendors nearby.

The gorge and bridge are about 11 miles west of Taos. From Taos Plaza, take Paseo del Pueblo 4 miles to the intersection of US 64 and Highway 150. Turn west and go 7 miles. And don't worry. You'll see the bridge in plenty of time. But you have to walk out onto it if you want to see the bottom of the gorge.

Izzat You, Art?

Taos

According to historians, Arthur Manby was not a well-loved person during his time in Taos in the 1920s. He was an unscrupulous and unprincipled scoundrel, so intensely disliked by those who dealt with him that few expressed sorrow when a decapitated body found in his home was identified as his.

The sheriff at the time declared that since there were so many people who hated Manby because of his shady dealings, he had way too many suspects, so he closed the case without arresting anyone. The lawman may have been partially justified in his actions because there was at the time—and still to this day—some doubt that the headless corpse was really Manby's. The speculation was that he had staged his own death to avoid the consequences of his dastardly deeds.

Either way, Manby is still a popular topic of discussion here because of the ghost.

Before the incident that may or may not have resulted in his death, Manby sold the building adjacent to his house to Dr. Thomas Martin, the namesake of the popular Doc Martin Restaurant in the Historic Taos Inn. Over the years, the restaurant kitchen has been the site of a variety of unexplained events. They include pots and pans flying off their hooks, canned goods falling off shelves, and an apparition of a man who allegedly resembles Manby staring at the workers. The figure, according to those who make note of such events, has also appeared in Room 109, which shares a wall with the kitchen.

Those who aren't fraidy cats can go see for themselves. The inn is at 125 Paseo del Pueblo Norte. Taking US 64, the inn is just south of Kit Carson Memorial State Park on the east side of the road. Or if you're not afraid of someone answering the phone with "whooooo is this?" call (888) 518-8267. But if you just want to take a peek, visit www.taosinn.com.

Saving the Planet Bottle by Bottle
Taos

When the people in charge of construction at Earthship need building materials, they don't go to a lumberyard or hardware store for 2-by-4's, reinforcing rods, or drywall. Instead they acquire items commonly found in dump grounds (now politically correctly referred to as "sanitary landfills").

So when the building project begins, the workers use discarded bottles, treadless tires, once-used metal cans, concrete, and a lot of dirt to convert throwaways into homes that they hope will help save the world. The buildings are self-sufficient, low-impact structures that rely heavily on recycling and nature. They harvest and recycle rain and groundwater, have their own contained sewage treatment operations, use solar and thermal power for heating and cooling, and get electric power from the sun and wind. The concept, known

Old tires and beer bottles are construction material at Earthship.

as Earthship Biotecture, has spread across the nation and around the world. One of its latest projects is under construction in the Caribbean Netherlands Antilles.

The Greater World Earthship Community is composed of a visitor center, permanent homes, and rental properties on 660 acres with 347 acres set aside as commonly owned open space. One of the rentals is the Phoenix Studio and Suite, a more advanced form of planet-saving housing. It contains 5,400 square feet and has three bedrooms, two bathrooms and WiFi Internet access. The entire house sleeps six, but small groups can stay in either the East Wing (sleeps four) or West Wing (sleeps two).

Architects, futurists, and the plain old curious folks can get there by taking US 64 west from Taos across the Rio Grande Gorge Bridge and following the signs for another 1.5 miles to the center on the right. There's a fee for roaming around the grounds on self-guided tours. For information, visit www.earthship.com or call (575) 751-0462.

It's Not Only In Humerica

Taos

The "Taos hum" is one of those things that get a lot of attention, but only certain people can hear it. Some say the hum is all in the ears of the hearer and pass it off as nonsense. But it has drawn international media notice and was once the subject of a congressional investigation.

In 1993 a group of Taos "hearers" (people who claimed they heard the hum) organized and demanded the lawmakers' probe. Dozens of scientists and observers from several prestigious research institutions came to study the situation. They interviewed 1,440 residents and concluded that 2 percent of them were hearers, but they weren't able to come up with anything definitive about what the hearers were hearing.

Those who said they heard the hum described it as a persistent low-frequency sound, something like a diesel engine idling in the distance. They said it occurred abruptly and was heard more often in buildings and cars than outdoors. A popular theory among the

Weird Names Abound

Beetchatuda Draw (a play on words), Gut Ache Mesa, Dirty Drawers Canyon, Five Dollar Canyon Creek, Fuzzy Mountain, Hard Cash, Lfd (a brand), Rough and Ready Hills, Stinking Spring, Werewolf Hill, Touch-Me-Not Mountain, and X-ray are all place names in New Mexico.

★ ★

hearers was that it was the caused by a military communications system used to contact submarines.

The government investigators discarded that possibility and then presented several possible answers—tinnitus (ringing in the ears), a background of electronic noise caused by technological advances, underground noise from plate tectonics, or electromagnetic waves caused by meteors.

Several Taos residents who professed to be non-hearers have a different explanation: "Some people just hear what they want to hear so they can get attention."

Similar hums have also been heard in the United Kingdom, Canada, and New Zealand. Nobody has yet explained them, either, but they make good fodder for the supermarket tabloids.

A Rock Ship of the Desert

Tesuque

Most of the time you have to squint, stand in exactly the right spot and/or use a lot of imagination to see the figure, shape, or face that's supposed to be represented in a rock formation. And then it usually doesn't look like what it's supposed to look like.

But not Camel Rock.

It is a big chunk of eroded sandstone that looks just like a camel, no matter how you view it. It has a hump, long neck, a big nose, and—when the sun's just right—flaring nostrils, just like those real ships of the desert that hang around the pyramids, circuses in Russia and zoos in America. Besides that, you don't have to hike across canyons and scramble down into gulches to see this creature of stone because it's about 40 feet high, and it's sitting right next to a major roadway north of Santa Fe.

Even better, you can drive your car right up to it because some wise person designated the area as Camel Rock Monument. There's plenty of parking right next to a stone walkway that leads directly to the beast. Getting there's easy: Take exit 175 off US 285.

A rock formation that can go years without water stands north of Santa Fe.

Because of it popularity, several nearby businesses and the pueblo's casino have incorporated Camel Rock into their names.

It's All In Who Tells the Best Story

Tucumcari

Nobody is absolutely certain about how this town got its name. But they sure have some interesting theories.

Some historians and linguists believe *tucumcari* was a Plains Indian term meaning "lookout point" or "signal peak." Others disagree. They say it is derived from *tukamukaru,* a Comanche word that loosely translates into "lie in wait for somebody or something to pass by." Both have substantial support in the nomenclature community because nearby Tucumcari Mountain was frequently used as a lookout by Comanche war parties. It was an excellent vantage point because scouts could look as far away as the Texas Panhandle some 50 miles away. And still another theory is that tucumcari can be translated from the Jemez language as "the place of the buffalo hunt."

But the story most people like best has nothing to do with linguistics or research. It's a sort of Romeo and Juliet tale created by a Methodist minister in 1907. His version involves Kari and Tocum, a pair of star-crossed young lovers. According to this version, Apache chieftain Wautonomah ordered Tonopah and Tocum, his bravest warriors, to fight to the death to determine which would succeed him. Tocum loved Kari and she loved him, but Tonopah won the fight. Overcome with grief and rage, Kari grabbed a knife and killed Tonopah herself.

Heartbroken that he had caused such a tragedy, the old chief stabbed himself and cried out, as he lay dying, "Tocum-Kari. Tocum-Kari." And the name stuck.

Or so the story goes.

Tucumcari is about a mile north of Interstate 40 on U.S. 54.

So Who's the Guy with the Big Head?
Tucumcari

If you're looking for somebody to be on your side the next time it looks like you're going to get into a bar fight, go find the guy who once wore that sombrero sitting on top of the La Cita Mexican Food restaurant in Tucumcari. If hat size is any indication, he is one big bruiser because this not a ten-gallon hat, it's more like a sixty-barrel hat.

But as you probably have already surmised, it's not a real sombrero. It's part of the eatery's signage. The giant hat sits on top of the building directly over the front door so nobody misses it. Brightly colored even to the point of being opulent, the headwear sits on an aqua building and measures some 12 feet from brim to brim and about that same distance from top to bottom.

★ ★

But don't be intimidated. The owner of the hat never comes to the restaurant because he wouldn't fit inside. Everyone else will find it at 821 North First Street, right on old Route 66. Take exit 322 off I-40 and go north on Highway 104. However, just to make sure that the big guy isn't there, call (575) 461-0944 and ask.

Some High-Class Dinosaurs

Tucumcari

Okay, so lots of museums have old dinosaur bones on display, complete with illustrated panels describing their original owners' eating habits and tiny brains. But do they have bones that are also works of art?

Not hardly.

Bronze replicas are cast from actual dinosaur skulls at the Dinosaur Museum in Tucumcari.

★ ★

It is that element that sets the Mesalands Community College's Dinosaur Museum apart because many of its dinosaur skeletons, bones, and skulls are exact replicas of the real things, but they're cast in bronze.

In 1997 the college established a dinosaur museum as part of its paleontology and geology programs, thereby becoming the only community college-affiliated museum in the country. The facility is housed in a 10,000 square foot building funded by donations and grants from individuals, organizations and government entities.

One segment of the museum's work involves the acquisition of ancient bones on a temporary basis, making casts, and then producing a bronze that is exact in every detail, right down to the tiny cracks in the creature's teeth. Among them are skulls of a saber-toothed tiger, an Ice Age lion, and a triceratops, plus the leg bone of a camarasaurus, a dinosaur in the same family as the brontosaurus that stands more than 8 feet in length. The centerpiece is a casting of a torvosaurus, a rare meat-eating dinosaur of the Jurassic period and similar to the *Tyrannosaurus rex.*

The bronzes are produced in the college's Fine Art/Bronze facility, using the lost wax method. And because they're metal, not resin or actual bone, it's okay to rub your fingers across them to sort of get a feel for what it was like on Earth millions of years ago. And, just in case you want one of your own but have some moral reasons for not trying to steal one from the display cases, the gift shop sells bronze replicas. (Actually, common sense may be the reason nobody tries to lift one rather than morals. Imagine, for example, trying to smuggle an 8-foot bronze camarasaurus bone past security.)

The museum, 222 East the corner of First and Laughlin Street, can be reached by taking exit 332 off I-40 and heading north on Highway 104/First Street. Turn right when you reach Laughlin, and the museum is on your right. Jurassic Park fans may get more information by visiting www.mesalands.edu/Museum/Museum.htm or calling (575) 461-3466.

Painting the Town Red . . . And Lots of Other Colors
Tucumcari

Sharon and Doug Quarles view this entire city as a personal canvas. So they're doing their best to cover it with paint, mostly in the form of murals.

More than thirty murals adorn Tucumcari. They're on grocery stores and fast-food outlets, a photography studio, and the chamber of commerce office. They depict history, trains, highways, cowboys, old cars, and pastoral scenes, and every one of them was painted by the Quarleses.

Their largest, a 14-by-114-foot tribute to Route 66, was applied to the east side of Lowe's Grocery. That one took nine months to complete, and the store held a dedication ceremony when it was unveiled. The Route 66 theme also appears on a McDonald's just down the street, where Ronald McDonald is depicted traveling along the fabled highway.

For another project, they wrapped an unearthly large rattlesnake around a water storage tank.

All this started in 2004 when the couple moved to Tucumcari. Their first effort was the result of a barter agreement. They used film cameras in their work at the time, and the owner of a photography store agreed to process their film in exchange for a mural. Now they either make proposals to other business places, or the merchants contact them and the process begins. And they still use cameras in the preliminary stages of their work so the results have a photo-realism sense.

The artists provide maps that show the locations of many of their works. Those interested can acquire one by stopping at the chamber office at 404 West Tucumcari Boulevard, sending an e-mail to chamber@tucumcarinm.com, logging on to www.quarlesart.com, or calling the chamber at (575) 461-1694 or the studio at (575) 461-7891.

★ ★

The Consummate Conestoga
Valle Escondido

The drive between Angel Fire and Taos is most pleasant because it features towering mountains, millions of trees, hundreds of winding curves, and a good variety of elevation changes.

And a giant Conestoga wagon that looks like it belongs in a sci-fi movie about 20-foot humans who came out to settle the West but left because they couldn't find 10-gallon hats big enough to fit them.

Perched on a hillside in the Enchanted Moon RV Park, the wagon measures about 15 feet high and 25 feet long, and the wheels are more than eight feet in diameter. But, as so often happens, it's not a real Conestoga wagon. Instead, it's a cabin built by Mike Moon, owner of the park. He lives in Lawton, Oklahoma, and needed a place to stay when he comes to visit his property so he constructed the Old West vehicle so he didn't have to sleep on the ground. He made it look like a Conestoga wagon because it reflects the traditions of the Old West.

It's quite comfy, a far cry from the real wagons that bore the early settlers. It has two bedrooms, living room, dining room, kitchen and indoor plumbing. The park, which rents 69 spaces, is closed from October 15 until May 1 every year. But the big Conestoga wagon is always there. There isn't a team of horses or oxen big enough to haul it away.

The establishment is on the south side of US 64 about 10 miles east of Taos.

A Tale in Tapestry
Villanueva

Stella Madrid unlocked the front door of Our Lady of Guadalupe Catholic Church and walked to a particular spot on the tapestry. "This is my part," she said, pointing to a section of the intricate work of art that encircles the interior of the church. It shows people

★ ★

riding horseback, a windmill pumping water into a tank, sheep graz-
ing, trees and birds, all assembled on a strip of white cloth. Below
the scenery, Stella stitched the name of her masterpiece—"El Dia de
Santa Anna."

She was one of thirty-six women from the town who worked for
two years creating the tapestry to celebrate the church's bicenten-
nial. The end result is the history of the community told in needle-
point. The tapestry is 265 feet long and 2 feet high and goes all the
way around the church. It starts at the back door, stretches alongside the pews and behind the altar, and even goes up into the choir
loft.

The work is magnificently rustic—delicate in some places, bold in
others. It depicts life in the village with such everyday scenes as farming, births, deaths, and historic events. One portion shows people
entering the church; another shows a baptism. There are customers
shopping at the local markets, and townspeople stopping by to visit
the neighbors. One segment entitled "Spanish Massacre" recalls a
dark episode in the town's past.

The church, an important part of Villanueva's history, was started
in 1790 but wasn't finished until 1830. It's the white building on the
west side of Highway 3 as it passes through the heart of the community, which is hidden away in some peaceful hill country about 12
miles south of I-25 and 20 miles north of I-40.

Pump-House Art

Villanueva

The tapestry in the church isn't the only depiction of this town's history. There's another version on the pump house.

Pump houses are usually ignored by artists and townspeople alike
because, for the most part, they're utilitarian edifices without much
charm. Not here. In this town of about 300 residents, the pump
house is a work of art, dedicated to those who brought water and
agriculture to the area.

It's a small building, maybe 10 feet by 10 feet and only about 6 feet tall. But it's striking because you just don't see many pump houses that tell a story in exterior paint like this one does in the mural wrapped around the structure. The building is identified at the top of the artwork as Villanueva Community Well. A rendition of a man takes up half of the front section. It's Pedro Gallegos, a town pioneer who helped bring the town's water system into existence more than a half century ago. As the painting unfolds around the sides of the building, it shows community and agricultural activities that exist because of the water, and the main street as it meanders through town. The work was done by area artist Janice Phelps.

Gallegos and his wife owned and operated the small grocery store just across the street for seventy-two years before his death in 2006. But the store remains open and in the family. Now it's run by Rosabel Gallegos, their daughter-in-law. The decorated pump house and the venerable store are both on Highway 3, a block north of the Catholic Church.

2

Northwest

Without a doubt, *northwestern New Mexico stands tall among upper left-hand regions of those states which are close to being perfect parallelograms. It is Utopia for those like me who seek out the curious, the quirky and the unique.*

For example, because of my journey through the northwest, I now count among my acquaintances a man who collects rattlesnake memorabilia, a woman who contorted herself in front of a large crowd so she could stand in four states simultaneously, and a man who built a huge sunflower out of bomb casings. A tattooed lady proudly displayed her skeleton sculptures. The owner of an outdoor barbecue stand gave me his business card, featuring a photo of him wearing only a necktie. This occurred shortly after I interviewed a woman who creates X-rated candy in her kitchen.

More than half the residents of New Mexico occupy space in Albuquerque. So do some rather weird buildings. One looks like a car tire, one has half a car sticking out of its front, and one resembles a semi-inflated balloon.

Unidentified flying objects are almost commonplace here in the northwest. There are believers, there are non-believers, and there are those who don't quite believe the non-believers. But they all have in common an almost-extinct talent for being nice to strangers. They gave directions, offered suggestions, and pointed out oddities. Most importantly, none of them gave me strange looks when I inquired as to the whereabouts of the world's tallest outhouse.

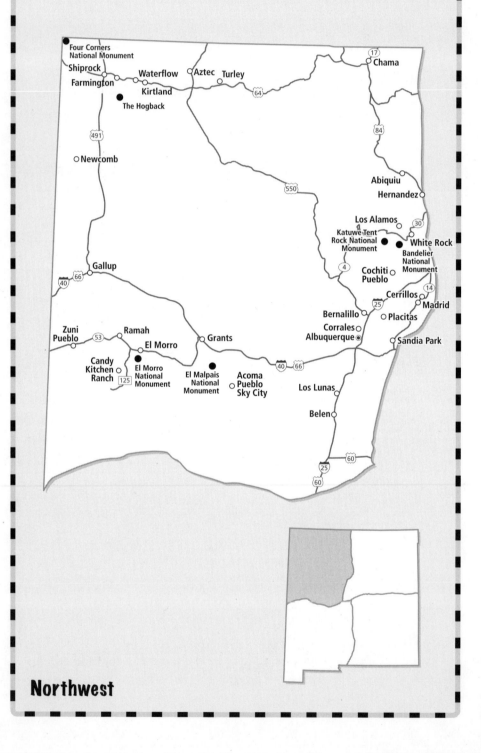

Four Corners
National Monument

Shiprock
Waterflow   Aztec   Turley
Farmington   Chama

Kirtland
The Hogback

491

Newcomb

Abiquiu
Hernandez

550

Los Alamos
Katuwe Tent
Rock National   White Rock
Monument
Bandelier
National
Gallup   4   Cochiti   Monument
40   66   Pueblo

Cerrillos
25   Madrid
Bernalillo   Placitas
Zuni   Ramah   Grants   Corrales
Pueblo   53   Albuquerque   Sandia Park
El Morro
40   66
Candy   El Morro
Kitchen   National   El Malpais   Acoma
Ranch   125   Monument   National   Pueblo
                                 Monument   Sky City   Los Lunas

                                             Belen

                                                        60
                                                  25
                                                        60

Northwest

Cast in Stone

Abiquiu

People who search the world for curious rock formations will find an El Dorado here because nature sculpted a variety of masterpieces and hid them in the surrounding hills. The weirdest is El Pedernal, a huge boulder that balances on a rock spire in such a precarious position that it must make onlookers wonder how much glue it takes to hold it there. It's about one mile to the north off U.S. Highway 84 as it passes through Abiquiu, but it is somewhat difficult to reach because the road is dirt, unmarked, and not very straight, so it's best to stop and ask for directions.

A few miles to the west, also off US 84, huge chunks of limestone and white sandstone rise dramatically from the surrounding high desert. The place is called Plaza Blanca and the formations resemble Grecian temples. Some of them are more than 100 feet high, and they're relatively easy to reach by taking Rio Arriba County Road 155 about six miles northwest off US 84, then turn north through a large gate made of telephone poles, and right where the dirt road meets pavement.

The land is privately owned but visitors are welcome as long as they don't climb on the rocks, wander off the designated trails, or take photographs for commercial use.

And then, also on US 84, 16 miles to the west, the Echo Canyon Amphitheater causes a lot of head turning and brake squealing because it looks so inviting. It's also sandstone, but the colors change as they scale up the sides, from red to yellow to white, sort of like somebody plopped a big scoop of spumoni ice cream on the spot and left it there to harden.

It's a large hollow, probably big enough to hold the Mormon Tabernacle Choir, a full orchestra, and a good-size crowd. It's on National Forest Service lands so there's a fee, but photo buffs and ice cream lovers can stop, drool, and take photographs on the entry road for free.

Strange rock formations abound in and around Abiquiu.

Since some of the formations are hard to find, it's best to stop at the Tin Moon Studio and Gallery in Abiquiu and ask for a free map. The studio is on the south side of US 84, right behind the post office.

Abiquiu is about 23 miles northwest of Espanola on US 84, in the midst of the Santa Fe National Forest. For more information call (505) 685-4829 or visit www.tinmoongallery.com.

A Very Isolated Temple

Abiquiu

The map from the Tin Moon Studio will also give directions to what the locals call "the mosque." Unlike the other items listed, this isn't a rock formation. It's a real mosque.

If it was located in a city or even a large town, it wouldn't be much of a rarity. But the Dar al Islam Mosque is way out there in the middle of nowhere, completely alone on the high desert amid the junipers.

Dedicated in 1981, the mosque is used as a retreat site more than a place of worship, and visitors are welcome to enter the prayer room for meditation. Those who take the time to visit will get a magnificent view of Abiquiu, the Chama Valley, the Sangre de Cristo Mountains, and the Santa Fe National Forest. Photos are allowed, but not for commercial use.

Getting there is easy, but the road is rather bumpy. Go through the same telephone-pole gate as the one used to access Plaza Blanca (it says Dar al Islam Mosque in big letters across the top and it's right where the paved and dirt roads meet), and then follow the signs. For more information, you can also visit www.daralislam.org.

Those who go there should remember, however, that it is a place of worship and deserves the proper respect. All visitors are asked to check in at the office before wandering around the grounds.

A Case of Legitimate Skullduggery
Abiquiu

One of the more recognizable icons associated with Georgia O'Keeffe is her painting of a white cow skull on a black background. One rendition of the skull hangs across the front gate of the Ghost Ranch, where the famed artist did some of her best work, while other versions appear on posters, brochures, and literature about the ranch.

But there is also a pair of the skulls hanging over a retirement complex in Tucson, Arizona, because of an act of kindness by O'Keeffe. In retrospect, the artist may have not liked the way her gift was used. However, true to her word, she never objected to its commercialization.

She created the skull in 1936 and then gave it—and the right to use it in any fashion—to Arthur Pack as a wedding gift. Pack owned the Ghost Ranch at the time, and O'Keeffe lived in a small house on the property. When Pack and his bride began wintering in Tucson, they opened a motel, named it the Ghost Ranch Lodge,

★ ★

and incorporated the cow skull into their signs. After the Pack family retired and sold the establishment, it remained vacant for several years and then was converted into a retirement facility. But the signs have remained through all the changes.

The motel/condo is at 801 West Miracle Mile in Tucson. See the next entry for more specific directions and information about the Ghost Ranch.

A Place for Old Bones
Abiquiu

New Mexico's Official State Dinosaur is the *coelophysis*, a paleontological name meaning "hollow bones." The reason it was given the high honor of being designated a state icon is that skeleton parts from more than 1,000 of them have been removed from the Ghost Ranch Quarry.

The first bone was discovered in 1947 when George Whittaker, a crew member from the American Museum of Natural History, stumbled across it protruding from some mudstone on the Ghost Ranch. The museum team was en route to Arizona from New York when they stopped to explore the property. After the find, 12 blocks of bones were removed and shipped to New York for study, and that made the quarry famous.

It also led to the creation of the Ruth Hall Ghost Ranch Museum of Paleontology, named for a woman who came to the ranch in 1961 and became an amateur paleontologist while exploring the red hills that dominate the area. The museum is built around Block 28, the last block taken from the quarry in 1985. Now visitors can watch the ongoing process of separating old bones from old stones in the museum and also check out the Ghost Ranch Quarry, a national natural landmark.

They may also visit the nearby Florence Hawley Ellis Museum of Anthropology, where exhibits display artifacts from Paleo Indian cultures of 10,000 years ago to the present time.

As dinosaurs go, the coelophysis was rather impressive because it stood 8 feet tall. But it apparently was a nice carnivore because researchers say it was graceful and used its forepaws as hands.

The Ghost Ranch is on US 84 about 10 miles northwest of Abiquiu. For more details about the various institutions and activities on the Ghost Ranch, call either (505) 685-4333 or (877) 804-4678, or log on to www.ghostranch.org.

No Work Here for a Logger
Acoma Pueblo

Under normal circumstances, it would take trained foresters using aerial photography and sophisticated computers a long time to count all the growth in a forest. But it's easy to enumerate all the trees in the Acoma National Forest: Just count to "one" and stop.

Obviously, there's a misnomer here. Forests have acre after acre of trees. The Acoma National Forest consists of a single cottonwood, standing forlornly on the mesa next to a waterhole. Also obviously, it's not a real forest. It's simply the name the residents of the pueblo jokingly use when they refer to the lonesome tree.

There were three trees when the "forest" was initially planted several years ago, next to a natural basin that collects rainwater. The other two didn't make it, but the survivor has toughed it out in a very unlikely and unnatural habitat. The pueblo is on top of a 375-foot mesa and the tree is about the only plant life growing there. Even weeds can barely eke out an existence on the platform because it's actually a big piece of sandstone.

Because of its location, Acoma Pueblo is perhaps better known as "Sky City." It was established atop the mesa about 2,000 years ago and claims to be the oldest continuously inhabited community in North America, although villages in Florida and Arizona also make the same statement. Besides the "forest," visitors to the pueblo can also inspect adobe houses, plazas and San Esteban del Rey Mission, completed about 1640. However, all guests must be

A lone tree is facetiously known as
the Acoma National Forest.

accompanied by an Acoma guide, and photographers need a special permit.

In 2007, Acoma Pueblo was named a National Trust Historic Site. A year earlier, the pueblo opened the Sky City Cultural Center and Haak'u Museum, a 35,000-square foot tourist center that gives visitors a taste of the pueblo's culture. To reach this "national forest," take exit 108 off Interstate 40 and drive south on Highway 23/Pareje Drive for about 12 miles to get to Acoma Pueblo. Details are available at www.skycity.com or call (800) 944-6487.

It's Not Easy Being a Rock
Albuquerque

The rocks that inhabit the landscape in the National Petroglyph Monument have been there for about 150,000 years. They have led a

★ ★

hard life. They've been sunburned, pecked, whacked, spied on from outer space, shot at, and vandalized over the ages, and people are still picking on them.

The boulders were deposited here by volcanic activity. The entire area emerged about 150,000 years ago when lava burst forth from a large crack in the earth's crust and flowed over and around existing landforms. Eons after the volcanoes stopped erupting, humans moved in. They discovered that chipping away the rocks' thin desert varnish revealed a lighter gray underneath and left a lasting mark. And so they began using the rocks as billboards and message centers, utilizing smaller rocks to scrape or peck away the dark brown sunburned surface of the boulders and inscribing them with signs and symbols called petroglyphs.

The original petroglyphers left and the rocks enjoyed a relatively peaceful time until about a half century ago, when a National Guard shooting range was established in the area and marksmen began using the ancient swirls and crosses for target practice. Next were the vandals, who began defacing the glyphs with spray paint and sharp instruments.

In an effort to combat the graffiti, park officials figured out a way to put most of the 20,000 petroglyphs on a Global Positioning Satellite matrix. With that eye in the sky, they use computers to locate any of the drawings and check them for vandalism.

In 2006 one of the big rocks was displaced by thugs who stole a pickup truck, drove it to the top of a ridge, and pushed it over the edge. The vehicle smashed into a petroglyphed boulder with such force that the big rock rolled down a hillside and came to rest on a concrete path, where it will probably stay because it's too heavy to move back up the hill.

Those who want to see what centuries of hard living will do can visit the monument by taking exit 154 off I-40 and then traveling 3½ miles north; then take Unser Boulevard until it intersects with Western Trail. Make a left at the light and go up the hill which leads to

★ ★

the visitor center about ¼ mile down the road. For more information, visit www.nps.gov/petrlog onto www.nps.gov/petr or call (505) 899-0205, extension 331.

Running Amok in the Muck
Albuquerque

Once every year, certain people here start thinking dirty.

And playing dirty.

They are participants in a rite of structured uncleanliness known as the Mudd Volleyball Tournament, held annually to raise money for the Carrie Tingle Hospital Foundation. The concept is simple: Get a lot of people together in a big mud hole, give them some volleyballs, and turn 'em loose.

This form of madness has been going on since 1994 and is now considered an Albuquerque icon. It draws more than 500 teams, who play on eighty-six muddy courts dug into a dusty field off Broadway Southwest near Rio Bravo. Since the mud is almost knee deep, such regular volleyball tactics as leaping and spiking are replaced by sloshing, falling, and getting mud up the nose.

The competition is made even tougher because when volleyballs get covered with slimy goo, they tend to get slippery and unmanageable. This, combined with a slippery playing field where the mud rises above the ankles, calls for completely different game strategies, including one that incorporates a return to the good old days when "here's mud in yer eye" was a common expression.

The event is held in late June and raises more than $300,000 every year. An estimated 12,000 spectators gather round to watch the amateur sloshers and mudders play in the muck. Teams entered in the 2008 competition included Mudd N' Roses, Weapons of Mudd Destruction and Muddy Amigos.

Got filth on your mind? Call the Albuquerque Convention and Visitors Bureau at (800) 284-2282 or contact the hospital foundation at (505) 243-6626 to find out if you're qualified.

One Odd-Shaped Building

Albuquerque

The Anderson-Abruzzo Albuquerque International Balloon Museum houses some big balloons and lots of historical data about big balloons. The museum is named for Albuquerqueans Maxie Anderson and Ben Abruzzo who, along with Larry Newman, completed the first manned balloon crossing of the Atlantic in 1978. Abruzzo and Anderson also did nonstop crossings of North America and the Pacific.

It's only natural, then, that the building itself would reflect its contents and so it does. The museum was designed to look like a partially inflated hot air balloon, with the entryway representing the mouth of the big bag. The interior rises up to wonderful heights, just like those big fabric bags do when the hot air is forced into them.

Beginning with the earliest European lighter-than-air experiments, the museum exhibits illustrate the development of recreational hot air and gas balloons, the use of balloons by the military, and the roles they have played in scientific and aerospace research.

Among the balloons on display are replicas of the first inflatable spheres used by the French aviators who pioneered this form of aerial entertainment, and the *Double Eagle V*, used for the flight across the Pacific. Visitors can also climb aboard a replica of the Double Eagle II, the first balloon ever to make a successful trans-Atlantic flight. Curiously, one famous balloon is missing. It's the one Dorothy Gale was supposed to take back to Kansas when she was scheduled to leave Oz.

Also inside the museum, youngsters scan test balloon fabric for strength, then assemble and launch mini-balloons in a special children's area, while adults can look out the huge windows and take in spectacular views of the adjacent Balloon Fiestaa Park with the Sandia Mountains in the background.

The museum is at 9201 Balloon Museum Drive. To get there, take exit 233 off Interstate 25 and go 1 mile west on Alameda Boulevard, turn right, and you will head straight to the parking lot. Lighter-than-air

A Governor with a Grasp

While campaigning for governor of New Mexico on September 14, 2002, Bill Richardson attended two major events in Albuquerque. His primary purpose was to gather support for his run for the state's highest elected office, but he wound up becoming an entry in the *Guinness Book of Records*.

While working the crowds who attended a New Mexico–Baylor football game in the afternoon and the New Mexico State Fair at night, Richardson was followed by a staff member armed with a counting device. Every time he shook someone's hand, the staffer clicked the clicker.

By the end of the day, Richardson had shaken 13,392 outstretched hands, the most ever by any politician over an eight-hour period. The feat earned him a sore hand that had to be iced down, a spot in *Ripley's Believe It or Not*, and the *Guinness Book* record.

Apparently, it also had the desired effect on the voters because seven weeks later, he was elected governor in a landslide.

fans and hot-air aficionados will receive more inflated information by logging on to www.balloonmuseum.com or by calling (505) 768-6020.

Another Odd-Shaped Building

Albuquerque

The Unser family came to the United States from Switzerland in the late 1800s and eventually became dominant figures in the sport of car racing. Marie and Louis Unser originally settled in Colorado

Springs where Louis started tinkering with gasoline engines. In 1915, the couple rode a motorcycle and sidecar to the summit of Pikes Peak, a mountain previously declared unreachable any way other than foot power.

The family's interest in car racing intensified when they moved to Albuquerque. Since 1934, when they started winning by putting the pedal to the metal, four generations of Unsers have won the India-napolis 500 nine times and finished first in the Pikes Peak race more than 50 percent of the time. They win in Colorado so often that the race is often called "Unsers' playground."

It's only natural, then, that the Unser Racing Museum would reflect that heritage, and so it does. The building that houses the museum was designed to look like the wheel of a car, lying on the ground. It's round, and the interior features a hub and six room divid-ers that represent spokes.

To carry the concept even further, the floor is made of recycled tires, some of the walls and ceilings resemble checkered flags, the soap dispensers in the men's restroom are shaped like miniature gas pumps, and the conference room is named Jerry's Garage, the name of the family's first automobile-related venture.

The Johnny Lightning car that once carried an Unser to victory at Indianapolis revolves in the hub of the giant wheel, and the rooms display other racing cars, a history of race-car engines, and a fam-ily genealogy. Four areas offer permanent exhibits and changing showcases.

Those who want to get a sense of making left turns while cruis-ing along at more than 200 miles per hour will find the museum at 1776 Montano Road. Take exit 155 on I-40 and go north on High-way 448/Coors Boulevard to the intersection with Montano Road. Go about 1.5 miles and the museum will be on your right. Don't be afraid to stop and ask for directions. But if the shame is too great, simply log on to www.unserracingmuseum.com or call (505) 341-1776.

★ ★

And Still Another Odd-Shaped Building
Albuquerque

El Torreon is a large round structure that sits at the entryway of the National Hispanic Cultural Center. It towers over the surrounding landscape, which is fitting because *torreon* is Spanish for "turret" and the building is 45 feet tall. And since it's also painted terra-cotta brown, it sort of resembles a chunk of frozen coffee that has slipped from its cup and landed upside down.

But any such frivolous image will vanish when Frederico Vigil finishes the masterpiece he's working on inside. He is painting a massive fresco that will eventually cover 4,300 square feet of wall and ceiling space. When completed, the work will trace centuries of Hispanic civilization and 300 years of Albuquerque history.

Vigil started the project in 2002 and doesn't expect to finish it until 2009. This is not an overly long period when painting frescoes. As an example, it took Michelangelo four years to paint the ceiling of the Sistine Chapel (1508–1512). The process dates back more than 5,000 years and involves the application of five layers of plaster. The first three layers can take up to ten days to dry before the final two layers can be added. The artist then paints on the final layer while it is still wet so the paint is absorbed into the damp surface.

Although the work is painstakingly slow, Vigil refuses to hurry the process because a mistake can be costly. One misstep with a brush and the entire section must be completely scraped off, replastered and repainted. Because of the need for caution, the artist said he isn't certain that the work will actually be finished in 2009.

All the colors and most of the figures are striking and bold. In one area near the top, Vigil has painted enormous hands that seem to be reaching inside the tower through a skylight. Halfway down the wall, a Madonna in gold-trimmed vestments stands beside a glowing sun while a newborn is lifted toward the heavens.

The tower will be open only during scheduled receptions until the artwork is completed but the center and its museums, located at 1701 Fourth Street, have regular schedules. Take exit 223 on I-25, and go west on Highway 314/Avenida César Chávez. At Fourth Street, turn south to the center. For more information, try www.nhccnm.org or call (505) 766-9858.

How 'Bout Them 'Topes?

Albuquerque

This city has had professional baseball off and on since 1880, and the teams have borne such athletic-sounding names as the Browns, the Dukes, the Dons, and the Cardinals. So why, with all the sports-related names available, did the current team wind up being called the Isotopes?

Isotope isn't a baseball name. An isotope is any of two or more species of atoms of a chemical element with the same atomic number and position on the periodic table and nearly identical chemical behavior but with differing atomic masses and different physical properties. What does any of that have to do with throwing strikes, scratching, running bases, eating hot dogs, and enjoying the seventh-inning stretching?

Blame it all on Homer Simpson.

The fictional baseball team in the popular television cartoon series *The Simpsons* is named the "Springfield Isotopes." They once threatened to move to Albuquerque until Homer went on a hunger strike and ultimately prevented the relocation. So when professional baseball returned to Albuquerque in 2003 after a two-year hiatus, the owners held a "Name the Team" contest, and 68,000 fans voted for the Isotopes to easily edge out such other entrants as Atoms, Dukes, Roadrunners, and 66ers. (Actually, Isotopes is not a bad name for Albuquerque, considering how much nuclear research is conducted in the immediate area.)

More importantly, the public seems to like it. Fans across the nation have bought up Isotopes merchandise with such fervor that it is one of the top ten best-sellers in minor league baseball.

★ ★

The Isotopes are affiliated with the Los Angeles Dodgers and play in the Pacific Coast League. And they have a mascot named Orbit, who stands 6 feet 5 inches and weighs 300 pounds. His favorite TV show is (did you really have to ask?) *The Simpsons*.

There's more of this sci-fi/Simpson/baseball scenario at www .albuquerquebaseball.com.

When Is a Bola Not a Bolo?

In the summer of 2007, after decades of anxiety and years of deprivation, New Mexico finally adopted official state neckwear. And it's not one of those frilly silk things that just dangles off the throat without making a statement. No, sir. It's the bola tie, an authentic symbol of the West.

Bolas, also known as string ties, feature a sliding clasp on a thin cord, often made of braided leather. The slides can be almost anything—gold, silver, copper, cactus, small animal skeletons, even plasticized horse droppings. The bola joins such other state icons as the bizcochito (official state cookie) and the roadrunner (official state bird).

Since they're relatively new to this form of attire, bola wearers should be cautioned when calling the neckwear a "bolo" tie. Some call it a bolo; however, a bolo is also a machete, used by some cultures to whack sugarcane, jungle growth, and, not infrequently, each other.

★ ★

An Unsuccessful Protest
Albuquerque

As protests go, the one here in 1984 was a sort of successful failure. It centered on Debbie Ball, also known as the Candy Lady, and the X-rated confections that saved her business.

Back in the early 1980s, Ball and her mother, Diana Garcia Davis, opened a small candy store and were having a tough time making it. Sales of their eight different kinds of candy weren't what they expected, maintenance was high and at one point they considered quitting. Then one day a customer told them about a store in New York that baked and sold naughty sweets, and Ball decided to try that approach. Her mother immediately and strenuously objected, but they reached a compromise—they'd make the X-rated delicacies but keep them in a refrigerator, away from the display cases. It was, Ball says now, a big mistake because they almost wore the hinges off the refrigerator door out by opening and closing it so often.

Word of the naughty niceties spread not only among her customers but also reached a church group, who organized a picket line. Only a couple of picketers appeared on the first day, but as many as 150 showed up with signs of protest the next day. They also asked the city to shut the business down.

But the protest backfired. The *Albuquerque Tribune* ran a front-page story about the incident, and that prompted national media coverage and an offer from the ACLU to defend the store owners. Deluged with adverse publicity about their cause, the picketers never came back.

The end result was that Ball and her mom had to work overtime to fill all the requests that came in immediately afterward, and the business was saved because of what she says was "$3 million worth of free advertising."

Her Candy Lady shop is located at 524 Romero NW on the corner of Mountain Road and Rio Grande Boulevard in Old Town (take exit 194 off I-40, and go south) at 524 Romero Street Northwest. Now she uses more than 5,000 different molds to make more than 500 different types of candy from thousands of recipes. And yes, among them are the ingredients for . . . ahem, well you know . . . those items in the special room with the big X on the door.

Due to a more relaxed attitude about things of a sexy nature, you don't have to wear a trench coat and fake eyeglasses attached to a rubber nose when you go into the store. But if you're still uncomfortable, call (505) 243-6239, place an order and have a liberated friend pick it up. For more information or to order online, visit www.the candylady.com or call (800) 214-7731.

His Place in Hiss-tory
Albuquerque

Basically, Bob Myers is an average person. He's a former high school biology teacher who followed his dream and now runs his own business in Old Town Albuquerque. So he's pretty normal, except for this one thing: He collects snakes and snakey things.

His enterprise, the American International Rattlesnake Museum, houses sixty-five slithery reptiles

Bob Myers collects many things related to rattlesnakes, including snake-bit license plates.

★ ★

gathered from a variety of places. Myers owns thirty-four different species of rattlesnakes and claims he has more species than the Bronx Zoo, Philadelphia Zoo, National Zoo, Denver Zoo, San Francisco Zoo, and San Diego Zoo combined, making his the world's largest collection, rattler-species-wise. But his place is more than Snakes on Parade. He has done extensive research on the creatures and can readily talk about snakes in history (Thomas Jefferson once proposed the timber rattlesnake as a national symbol), the movies (one wall is covered with posters from such movies as *Anaconda*), and humor (the welcome sign on his front door says, "Slither Right In").

One portion of the museum is devoted to snake-related liquid refreshments including booze. Myers has assembled more than 150 bottles and cans with names like King Cobra Ale, Grand Canyon Rattlesnake Beer, Snake Venom Cola, Black Adder Scotch, Mamba Beer, and Snake Eyes Wine. Another area shows how easily the reptiles have snaked their way into the automotive culture because the wall is covered with personalized license plates like "Snakebit" from Iowa, "Serpent" from Oklahoma, and "Ven U Mus" from New York. Myers's own plates say "Rattler."

The museum is located at 202 San Felipe Northwest. (Take exit 157A off I-40 and head south on Rio Grande, turn left on Mountain Road, and in one block, on your left will be San Felipe.) Myers is looking for a larger place because, he says, only 2 percent of his collection is now on display. Those in need of a herpatology fix can log on to www.rattlesnakes.com or call (505) 242-6569.

A Face in the Tree
Albuquerque

There's a very old cottonwood tree rising from the courtyard next to San Felipe de Neri Church. Ordinarily, it wouldn't draw much attention, other than a casual notation that it's quite large, and the fact that it's on The National Register of Historic Places. But those who walk around the tree and look at the side not visible from the

★ ★

A grateful Korean War veteran carved a statue of the Blessed Virgin after returning from battle.

street will spot a figure of a woman clad in blue emerging from the trunk.

It's a wooden statue of the Virgin of Guadalupe, and the figure is actually whittled into the tree trunk. It was carved more than fifty years ago by Toby Avila, a parish member. Avila was on active duty in the U.S. Navy during the Korean Conflict and vowed that if he returned home safely, he would create an image of the Blessed Virgin to show his gratitude.

Using only a kitchen knife and a flashlight, Avila chipped away at the tree trunk for a year before the statue was finished. He had to do the carving and painting at night because he also had a full-time day job. And then, two days after he completed the task, Avila died. There was still blue paint on his hands as his body lay in state in the church.

The church, erected in 1793 to replace the original mission church built in 1709, is at 2005 North Plaza Street in Old Town Albuquerque, which is off San Felipe Northwest (see article above). And since the carving was done more than a half century ago, the bark of the tree has grown around portions of it. But the major part of it remains visible.

To reach the sculpture, go through the garden area on the north side of the church and out into the parking lot.

Take a Byte Out of This, Apple

Albuquerque

Microsoft didn't start in Seattle or the Silicon Valley. Bill Gates and Paul Allen programmed the Altair 8800 in Albuquerque back in 1970. In those times novice computer geeks could order an Altair kit through the mail for a mere $397, but when it arrived, they had to put it together themselves with a soldering iron.

Now the original Altair sits on a revolving pedestal, lit up like the crown jewels in the New Mexico Museum of Natural History and Science as part of a permanent exhibit honoring the pioneers. It's entitled "Startup: Albuquerque and the Personal Computer Revolution." While tracing the history of the computer, the placards note that a person needed $35,000 per month to rent one in 1973, and it would require enough electricity to power a small town. By 1975, however, they were on sale . . . for $20,000 each.

But for those interested in space stuff, there's an even more interesting display elsewhere in the museum. It's a scale model of the universe, featuring all eight planets. In this mock-up, Jupiter is a sphere about 6 feet in diameter, while Earth and Mars are similar, about the size of softballs. Pluto isn't included, and that's understandable in view of the 2007 downgrading of that celestial body from planet to dwarf star. But that's not the reason the ex-planet isn't depicted. Even though the model is, on a scale of, say, one-billionth actual size, Pluto would still be somewhere around Santa Fe, some 75 miles away.

Feeling pretty important? Go see just how small we are. The museum is at 1801 Mountain Road Northwest. (Take exit 157A, and go south on Rio Grand. Turn left on Mountain Road, and the museum is on the left across from Tiquex Park.) You can't miss it because there are life-sized dinosaurs standing guard at the front entrance. Log on to www.NMnaturalhistory.org or call (505) 841-2800 for hours and fees.

George in Turquoise
Albuquerque

Nearly everyone has heard the stories about faces that miraculously appear on pancakes, bread, tortillas, plants, and even animal hides. Most of them are usually religious figures, and that factor makes the face in the Museum of Turquoise a curiosity of the highest magnitude.

It's George Washington.

The profile of the nation's first president is outlined on a 6,800-carat turquoise nugget mined from Turquoise Mountain, and it bears a striking resemblance to the profile that has adorned U.S. quarters for decades. Displayed beneath an American flag alongside some information about Washington and turquoise, it's the only stone like it anywhere in the world.

The Museum of Turquoise itself is also a bit unusual because of its location. Most institutions of its kind are housed in separate buildings with lofty foyers, towering atria and big display cases. But this one is in a storefront shop behind a Walgreens Drug Store. This has its advantages, however. Joe Dan Lowry, one of the owners, can honestly say that place is "the world's best turquoise museum located in a strip mall."

Those who go to the museum enter through a fake mine shaft to view the many varieties of turquoise collected from all over the world, and read about how turquoise, on a pound-for-pound basis, is much rarer than diamonds. Guides, often Lowry himself, conduct tours and willingly go into detail about what makes one piece of turquoise more valuable than another. (Hint: It has a lot to do with the mine it comes from, not the size). They also explain what makes one piece of turquoise jewelry better than another.

A large piece of turquoise bears a striking resemblance to the Father of Our Country.

Turquoise enthusiasts and George Washington Fan Club members will find the museum at 2107 Central Avenue. Take exit 157A off I-40, and go south until you hit Central Avenue/Historic Route 66; the museum is on the corner. For details, call (505) 247-8650.

★ ★

The Ghost's Revenge
Albuquerque

After the plans for the National Hispanic Cultural Center had already been drawn up, the planners started the property acquisition process. By 1998 all the necessary land had been purchased except for two small houses on lots owned by a woman in her late eighties. She had lived there her entire life and didn't want to sell.

Officials begged, cajoled, and threatened. She wouldn't sell. Local politicians brought pressure. She wouldn't sell. They offered her two new homes. She wouldn't sell. They appealed to her relatives. She wouldn't sell. Then the local media heard about the situation and the woman began appearing on television and in newspapers, telling her side of the story while leaning on her walker.

The issue was resolved when those in charge of the project decided to go back to the drawing board rather than let the discord go on. It cost them $250,000 for a new set of plans and the center was built right next to, and almost encircling, the two little houses.

The elderly woman died before the project was completed. But there are those who believe she's still having the last word. When the center opened, people started reporting that they had seen the ghost of a woman roaming the halls, first in the History and Literary Arts Building then in the Disney Theater. And there are reports of lights being mysteriously turned off and on, items being moved, and eerie sounds.

It's never anything serious, and the presence never bothers the visitors who tour the Intel Center for Technology and Visual Arts, the art museum, the computer learning lab, or the Roy E. Disney Center for the Performing Arts, all part of the center.

Is it the ghost of the elderly woman? Nobody's saying for sure. Only that there seems to be something unexplainable going on and she's a logical candidate when it comes to pointing a finger.

Casper fans and ghost busters alike can visit the center at 1701 Fourth Street Southwest (take exit 223 on I-25 and go west on

Avenida César Chávez to Fourth). For details, log on to www.nhccnm
.org or call (505) 246-2261.

One Tiny Church

Albuquerque

The Chapel of Our Lady of Guadalupe is not only the smallest church
in the city, but it's also the only privately owned church in the city.

It was built by Sister Giotto, who owned the land, in memory of
the Blessed Virgin's appearance to a Mexican shepherd in the 1800s
and was consecrated by the archbishop of Albuquerque, and for
many years a local priest said mass there. But when the priest was
transferred, the services stopped and Sister Giotto sold the property.
Numerous inquiries failed to turn up the name of the new owners, but whoever they are they keep the small building in excellent
condition.

The chapel holds only about a dozen people and has no pews.
Those attending mass had to sit on small benches along the walls in
the altar area, one of the two rooms contained in the structure. The
other room is also small, just big enough to hold some statues and
candles.

Open daily to the faithful and sightseers, the chapel is located
on the east side of San Felipe Road between Charlevoix and Church
streets. (Off I-40, take exit 157A and go south on Rio Grande, make
a left onto Mountain Road, and in 1 block, turn left onto San Felipe.)

The Great Smoke Hoax

Albuquerque

Albuquerque isn't exactly a basin, but the city is well flanked by such
major geological formations as mountains and large hills. They include
the Sandia Mountains to the east and five extinct volcanoes lined
up along the western horizon. That quintet of former lava gushers
became the center of an elaborate hoax more than a half century ago.

Where'd You Get That Name?

The city of Albuquerque was named after "El Duke de Alburquerque," who was the viceroy of New Spain at the time the city came into existence. But the sharp-eyed will notice a disparity in the spelling. Apparently worried about a high incidence of misspelling, the city's founding fathers dropped the first r back in the 1800s. It didn't help much. According to a nonscientific survey, Albuquerque is spelled wrong just about as often as Tumacacori, Arizona; Ypsilanti, Michigan; and Copperopolis, California.

The Sandia Mountains that flank Albuquerque's eastern border got their name because they looked edible. The Spanish soldiers who explored the region observed that the mountains took on a pinkish hue at sunset, so they called them *sandia*, the Spanish word for "watermelon."

The Spanish were also responsible for giving Tesuque Pueblo its name. The site was originally called *tay tsugeh oweengeh*, a Tewa phrase meaning "village of the narrow place of cottonwood trees." Apparently, early Spanish explorers had trouble pronouncing that, so they shortened it to "tesuque."

One morning back in 1947, residents all over Albuquerque awoke to the smell of smoke and a western sky that was discolored by a red haze. Even worse, the smoke was coming from Vulcan Volcano, the tallest of the five. And it wasn't just smoke; it was a thick black smoke. Even worse than that, some frightened folks said there were two volcanoes spewing the black clouds.

Although the volcanoes had been quiet for thousands of years except for a brief smoke-puffing episode in the 1880s, the black cloud was enough to alarm Albuquerqueans, especially when local media ran stories indicating that an eruption could be coming. This caused a certain amount of panic and officials considered evacuating everyone. Some people didn't wait for the order to leave and actually did flee the city.

The fear may have been based on a scientific report that the area around Albuquerque remains potentially active because it sits on the Rio Grande Rift, so a new volcano could erupt somewhere along the rift.

But calmer heads prevailed, and a few curious souls climbed to the top of the volcano and peered over the rim to see what was causing the ruckus. What they found was not fire and brimstone, but a burning pile of old rubber tires. Further investigation revealed it was all a prank staged by students from the former St. Joseph's College. Apparently, the collegians had hauled the tires up the volcano under the cover of darkness, doused them with gasoline, and lit them.

In the years that followed, the stunt was emulated several times by other college students, but none of the other pranks had the impact of the first one.

You Want Fries with That Taurus?
Albuquerque

The sign on the front of the Mustang Cafe looks like somebody drove a vintage Mustang convertible through the wall on the second story, and then simply left it there to go have lunch. It's a fake Mustang, but it sets the tone for the establishment because it's located in an automobile dealership and most of the menu items have car-related names.

Once the hungry masses, the snackers, and the empty-tummied walk through the entrance, they immediately notice that the walls are covered with Mustang artwork and photographs that honor one of the more successful cars ever produced by Ford.

★ ★

The Mustang Cafe offers tortillas and Ford art in Albuquerque.

A coffee shop had been in the Rich Ford auto complex for several years, but it didn't become the Mustang Cafe until Cecelia Saavedra bought it, moved it downstairs, and gave it the name. Now she serves items named after Ford models, like the Super Duty F529 (a chile relleno, tamale, cheese enchilada, and soft taco), the Explorer (tamales, tacos, and enchiladas), and several other dishes with similar designations—the GT Ranger, Taurus, Crown Victoria, Focus, and Excursion. And, of course, the obvious one—the Mustang (a chile-laden burger wrapped in a tortilla). Not surprisingly, there's no Edsel on the menu.

Customers sit on stools covered with Ford logos to give them better vantage points for critiquing the artwork while they scarf down the food.

Rich Ford and the Mustang Cafe are located at 8601 Lomas Boulevard Northeast (take exit 164 off I-40 and head south). The phone number is (505) 275-4477, but don't call and ask for a Model T-bone. It's not on the menu, either.

Home of the Nice Soreheads
Aztec

The signs leading into town say WELCOME TO AZTEC. HOME OF 6,378 FRIENDLY PEOPLE AND 6 OLD SOREHEADS. The signs were put up several years ago. Between then and now, the number of friendly people has since grown to slightly more than 7,000 but there are still only six old soreheads.

That's because being a sorehead in this town is actually an honor, not denigration. Only residents who have a strong interest in community affairs (and a good sense of humor) can be selected for the dubious distinction. A slate of potential soreheads is announced about midway through the year and the winners are elected by voters who toss coins into each candidate's collection cans. Then the six winners get to wear paper sacks over their heads until they are "unveiled" as the new Old Soreheads during an Oktoberfest parade.

To make sure they know how to conduct themselves during the coming year, each sorehead gets a copy of an instruction manual

A Case of Misplaced Fame

The Roswell Incident, in which an alien spacecraft allegedly crashed, didn't happen in Roswell. The debris, later identified by the U.S. Air Force as a weather balloon, was actually found near Corona, a small ranching community more than 80 miles northeast of Roswell. But Corona didn't have a military base nearby and Roswell did so all the investigation and news reports came out of Roswell.

★ ★

entitled "How to Be an Old Sorehead." It doesn't say anything about grumpiness, grousing around, causing stomach upset, snarling at little children, tipping less than 2 percent, or frowning. Instead, it lists nice things like getting involved in the community and how to help people less fortunate.

The tradition started in 1969 and all the money contributed in the form of votes goes to support community projects. But it hasn't always received full support from the townspeople. Since 1970, city officials (also referred to as "those wet blankets") have made two stabs at getting rid of the tradition and the signs but have been voted down both times.

Grousers, grumblers, and sorehead wannabes can get more information at www.aztecchamber.com.

Who Were Those Little Men?

Aztec

Roswell's UFO incident gets most of the publicity and attention but many other similar reports have been made all across New Mexico. One allegedly occurred near Aztec on March 25, 1948, and is still a topic of discussion among people who study such things and gather here annually to discuss that very subject.

The story goes as follows: A disc measuring about 100 feet in diameter allegedly landed near Aztec and sixteen alleged small humanoids, measuring from 36 to 42 inches, were allegedly found dead inside. The spacecraft allegedly was undamaged and allegedly made of a metal so durable that even a diamond-tipped drill couldn't penetrate it. Allegedly, as soon as the federal government heard about it, personnel from an airbase in Colorado raced to the area, roped off the alleged crash site, loaded the alleged craft and the alleged bodies into camouflaged trucks, and hustled them back to a secured area. No official statements were ever released by the government.

But even after more than sixty years, speculation remains high that something out of this world actually happened that day. The case has been the subject of two books and both authors claimed they had uncovered conclusive evidence that the crash *did* occur, and that the crew *was* composed of little beings. Skeptics say it ain't so and produce evidence to show that it was all a scam engineered by two Colorado con men trying to sell outer space stuff.

The alleged crash site is about 30 miles northeast of downtown Aztec (off Main Street/U.S. Highway 550, turn onto West Chaco and go two blocks to Ash). And, while the city doesn't promote the episode, it does distribute free maps showing the location, and it has hosted a UFO Symposium every year since 1999. The maps are available at the Visitor Center, 110 North Ash. For more information, call (505) 334-9551 or log onto www.aztecchamber.com.

High-Rent District?
Bandelier National Monument

So you think renting a new high-rise apartment makes you a trendsetter? Well, it's actually not that big a deal. The folks who lived here were doing it more than 700 years ago.

The ancient Puebloans who settled in the area not only built stone houses and kivas but also dug caves into the tuff stone that had been deposited by volcanic eruptions more than a million years ago. The caves served as ideal residences and storehouses because they stayed cool in the summer and warm in the winter. Even though the tuff is relatively soft, carving into it was difficult because the carvers had only stone tools.

The lower walls were usually plastered with mud then painted using native plants as dyes. The ceilings, however, were soon blackened by smoke from the cooking and heating fires inside the caves. The smoke hardened the ceilings and made them less crumbly.

Now visitors to the monument can scramble around in the caves, once they pay the entry fee and take a short hike. The first complex was dug into a huge chunk of tuff, and some of the makeshift homes are as much as 30 feet above ground. Access is by wooden

Tourists can scramble around in ancient second-story
housing units in Bandelier National Monument.

ladders propped against the openings but amateur spelunkers
should be forewarned of a problem: The ladders are crude, not at
all like those on sale at your friendly neighborhood hardware store.
The rungs are much farther apart so it takes a series of large steps
to reach the top. And then comes the hard part—getting back
down.

The Old Ones who built the ladders might have been able to scoot
up and down them without fear, but today's climbers have to make
their retreats the same way babies climb down stairs—backward and
very slowly.

The monument is four miles southeast of White Rock on Highway
4. For more information, call (505) 672-3861 or log on to www.nps
.gov/band.

Where the Lions Don't Roar

Bandelier National Monument •

There are three stone lions within the boundaries of this natural wonderland. Two are bas-relief representations carved into the rocks; they can be viewed by the public. The third is a full-scale replica also carved in stone but hidden in a secret place after a near-fatal encounter with humans.

No one knows for certain who carved them or when they were carved. Speculation centers on fertility rites of the ancient Puebloans who inhabited the region more than 1,000 years ago. They had lain in the same spot until 1970, when a team of anthropologists from the University of New Mexico decided to move the large one for its own protection.

The lion's whereabouts had been a poorly kept secret for years. Vandals were among the first to find it, and they did considerable damage so the anthropologists figured it would be better off in a museum.

After obtaining permits from the Cochiti Pueblo, the team arrived at the scene with four-wheelers, ropes, iron pipes, steel bars, an old mattress, and other equipment required to dislodge the stone lion. But things didn't go well. One team member was injured when a boulder fell on him. The others had to scramble up sheer cliff faces dotted with glasslike obsidian that hacked their arms and legs.

Finally, however, they pried the stone figure loose, strapped it with nylon cords, and called for the helicopter they had rented to haul it off the mesa. Then there were more problems. The flatbed truck needed to haul the lion back to Albuquerque ran out of gas so it was late getting to the dropping-off point. While attempting to set the lion down on the truck, the helicopter raised so much dust the ground crew couldn't guide the descent properly, and the copter released the lion prematurely, dropping it on the flatbed rather than easing it down gently.

Fortunately, no damage resulted and the lion was trucked to a back lot on the UNM campus. And it sat there for the next eleven years because there was more trouble.

The residents of San Felipe Pueblo claimed the lion belonged to them and they wanted it back. And non-council members of the Cochiti Pueblo said they hadn't been told the sculpture would be moved so they wanted it put back. It took an act of Congress (the 1981 Native American Religious Freedom Act) to settle the issue. The stone lion was returned to its original site and this time the helicopter ride was uneventful.

Now it lies hidden in obscurity, hopefully safe from vandals armed with rifles and spray paint. The entire story is wondrously told in the book *Mysteries and Miracles of New Mexico* by Jack Kutz. Although the big lion is not available for public inspection, the two smaller ones may be viewed, but it's a long and rugged trek into the interior of Bandelier, so ask for directions at the park headquarters before making the attempt.

Perpetual Nativity
Belen

The city was founded by Spaniards Don Diego Torres and his brother-in-law, Antonio Salazar. They named it Belen, Spanish for Bethlehem, in honor of the birthplace of Christ. So it's only natural that a Nativity scene would be an integral part of the landscape.

The difference here is that the Belem Nativity doesn't get taken down and stored away after Christmas. It's there permanently, sitting under a new archway in a community park known as the Heart of Belen at the intersection of Becker, Dalies, and Main streets (on I-25, take exit 191 and go east, until you hit Main, where you turn left).

The figures were cut from ¼-inch steel plates that are gently rusting as they age. They include the basics—the Baby, Mary, Joseph, camels, shepherds, wise men, cows, and sheep. There's no admission fee to pause and reflect in a pleasant slice of open space.

Also in Belen, at the bottom of Tome Hill east of town, there stands a sculpture paying tribute to the importance of the El Camino Real Trail, one of the oldest and most important historic trails in the nation. Figures in the sculpture, done by New Mexico artist Armando Alvarez, represent people who were part of the trail and the area's history. It's called *Puerta del Sol* (door of the sun). Tome Hill is also the site of Belen's annual Good Friday pilgrimage.

Equally interesting is an old Harvey House, built in the early 1900s as part of the extensive restaurant system established by Fred Harvey to feed railroad passengers. This one is a rarity because most of the Harvey Houses were demolished when railroad passenger service ended. Located at 104 First Street, it's now owned by the city and houses a museum operated by the Valencia County Historical Society.

Belen is about 35 miles south of Albuquerque on I-25.

Burning Their Cares Away

Belen

Got troubles? Bring 'em to Belen in August and watch them go up in smoke.

For more than 200 years, residents have held the annual Our Lady of Belen Fiesta, which draws crowds of up to 8,000, both locals and visitors. The fiesta activities include a queen contest, chile contests, music, dancing, and cash giveaways in which the grand prize winner can take home as much as $10,000.

While all that's going on, fiesta organizers prepare Old Man *Quejas* (Problems) for his fate, which is a fancy way of saying he's going to meet a fiery end. Residents work for months building the 26-foot tall papier-mâché figure. They provide not only the labor, but also the materials, mostly shredded paper collected by the city, county and schools. When they're done, the symbolic old man gets transported to a town square where people write their troubles on pieces of paper and put them into a box next to the soon-to-be-torched model.

★ ★

Once the local Fire Department says the situation is good to go, the figure gets lit up, literally. The onlookers cheer as their problems are devoured by the flames, and everyone lives happily ever after, at least until the next year.

Those who wish to unburden themselves in this manner rather than go through therapy can get more information by visiting www .belenchamber.com or by calling the Belen Chamber of Commerce, (505) 864-8091.

A Bar for All Mankind
Bernalillo

The Silva Saloon is one of those places you hear stories about, but you always wonder if they really exist or are merely the illusions visualized by beer-soaked brain cells. This is because bars like this are such one-of-a-kind places that when other bars try to emulate it, they rarely succeed because they have neither the right amount of showmanship nor the proper number of artifacts.

It's not so much the bar itself; it's the décor. The bar is a common octagon shape, made of hardwood and aged by decades-old applications of spilled suds, weary elbows and tales of misunderstanding spouses. A couple of strategically placed peanut-dispensing machines offer sustenance and a friendly barkeep keeps the brews flowing, just like the thousands of other bars that serve as gathering places for the thirsty, the tired and the misunderstood.

But the walls, the ceilings, and every other available space are what make the Silva Saloon a curiosity because they are covered with things. Funky stuff; things nobody really needs but would really like to have. Like license plates and old lanterns, cowboy boots and baseball caps. Nude paintings, old photographs, dollar bills, saddles, antique toy cars, a device for administering beer intravenously, neon signs that still work, life-size pinups, jewelry, skulls, canes, bells, old whiskey bottles, pins and jukeboxes, to name but a few.

The saloon opened in 1931 and is the oldest family-owned bar in New Mexico. Felix Silva Sr. started it and when he died, his son, Felix Jr., took over and still runs it, with help from his daughter, Denise Silva. And it was elevated to a place of high distinction in 2007 when it was named to *Esquire Magazine's* list of the "Best Bars in America," the only establishment of its kind in New Mexico to be so honored.

Anyone with a hankerin' to take a trip down Memory Lane, put a nickel into a nickelodeon, gaze at an Elvis decanter, or just have a cold beer will find the saloon at 955 Camino del Pueblo in downtown Bernalillo, phone number (505) 867-9976. Take exit 240 off I-25 and head west on Avenida Bernalillo to where it intersects with Camino del Pueblo. Head north and the bar is on your left.

A Half a Caddy Is Better than None

Bernalillo

Tourists who stop at the old Sandoval County Visitors Information Center can have their picture taken in a half a Cadillac. Or what looks like a real Cadillac, depending on which angle the photographer uses to snap the shot.

Once comfortably seated, tourists and the make-believe *nouveau riche* wave and pretend they're living in luxury while riding around in an expensive automobile that probably cost more than they earned in a year. But in actuality, they are sitting on wooden benches cleverly placed behind a tin replica of a high-priced vehicle. The cutout, which represents only the passenger side of the car, was created by Jake Lovato, a local metalworker. It's a vintage Caddy, painted teal blue and featuring those wonderfully decadent fins from those glorious days when cars were real cars that didn't have to worry about $160-a-barrel oil and air quality as they belched their way across the country at 8–10 miles per gallon.

And the nice thing about it is that, even though it's phony, there's no charge for taking part in an illusion.

The visitor information center still gives out free maps and brochures but in a new location. In the summer of 2007, the agency moved across the street into an old convent at 264 Camino del Pueblo. But the half Cadillac is still at the old site, which has been converted into an art gallery. Those who want to live in this type of fantasy high style without paying for it will find this photo op at 243 Camino del Pueblo. Take exit 242 and head west on US 550 until you reach Camino del Pueblo. Turn left and go about 2 blocks. The center is on your right and the Caddy on your left.

Tourists who stop at Bernalillo can have their pictures taken in a fake luxury car.

Bernalillo is 18 miles north of downtown Albuquerque. From I-25, take exit 240, then go west on Avenida Bernalillo and turn right on Camino del Pueblo. If you still can't find it, call (800) 252-0191 or log onto www.sandovalcounty.com.

And have a nice trip in the Caddy, even though you're not going anywhere.

A Howling Sanctuary

Candy Kitchen Ranch

Leyton Cougar would probably get a lot of inquiries about his last name even if he was a computer nerd or a college professor or a professional athlete. But the questions become inevitable upon learning what Cougar does for a living: He saves wolves.

Cougar is the executive director of Wild Spirit Wolf Sanctuary, a nonprofit organization dedicated to rescuing abandoned and abused wolves and wolf-dogs, providing them with permanent and safe quarters, and educating the public that, despite what Red Riding Hood says, wolves are not horrible creatures that scarf down grannies.

Many of the salvaged wolves are brought to the site because unscrupulous breeders profit from the belief that if a wolf puppy is raised like a dog, it will act like a dog when grown. It's a falsehood of the highest order, made even worse because captive-bred wolves have no experience in their natural environment and therefore cannot be released into the wild once the owner realizes the mistake.

The sanctuary keeps about sixty wolves on its property, where they form pairs or family groups that live in wooded compounds ranging from 5,000 square feet to a full acre. None come directly from the wild. They were usually captive bred and then sold to people who mistakenly assumed they could raise a wolf as a pet. When they find out they can't, they turn to the sanctuary. So workers get up to seven calls per day asking for help in disposing of the unwanted animals.

Besides caring for the creatures, the facility offers guided tours that start in front of a wood-burning stove in a hogan-style gift shop, or an overnight camping experience with the background music provided by the night howls of the wolves. Photography tours are also available. Those interested should call ahead for reservations.

The preserve is a mountainous area south of U.S. Highway 53 between Ramah and El Morro. From Ramah, go 10 miles east on US 53 to BIA 125, then turn right and go 8 miles (through Mountainview).

★ ★

Turn right onto gravel road BIA 120. You will find Wild Spirit Wolf Sanctuary 4 miles down on the left. For more information, log on to www.wildspiritwolfsanctuary.org or call (505) 775-3304.

Saving the Branches

Cerrillos

Some guys look at dead tree branches and envision slingshots. Others see them as material that belongs in a glowing fireplace. And a few might convert them into walking sticks, makeshift baseball bats, or even, in rare cases, cudgels.

But give Ken Wolverton a tree branch and he sees an elk.

He can turn just about any piece of wood into a work of art. A life-size elk composed of aspen branches stands at the front gate of his

Ken Wolverton uses the whole tree
when he creates his art.

studio. The one in his downtown gallery was crafted from branches he rescued from a friend who had to cut down several apple trees after they died. He created fifteen animals from that windfall, and one of his elks wound up in a private residence in Denver.

Wolverton also uses plywood, driftwood, junk wood, discarded construction lumber, and any other wood as long as it's cheap and there's plenty of it. Then he turns it into what he calls "well-organized firewood." He holds the creatures together with heavy gauge wire instead of wooden pins for two reasons:

First, the wire is more flexible. Second, he got a 1,000-foot roll of wire for nothing.

Wolverton's background hardly indicates a life as a scrounger, however. He created public art in Turkey and Iran in 1977, a sculpture for the beautification of St. Mary McCullop in Australia in 1995, graduated magna cum laude from the University of Arizona with a degree in journalism in 2004, then became an honor student at New Mexico State University the following year.

His work is on display all over New Mexico, ranging from an eight-panel ceramic tile work in Las Cruces to a three-horse wooden sculpture in a bar in Madrid. His studio is just north of Cerrillos. Take exit 276 off I-25 (276A if you are coming from the southwest), and go about ½ mile on Veteran's Memorial Highway. Turn right onto Highway 14 and follow it about 14 miles south. Some of his work is also displayed at In Cahoots, a gallery in Madrid. For more information, contact Wolverton at kjwolverton@aol.com or call the gallery at (505) 438-3439.

A Bistate Transport

Chama

It's not the fact that the Cumbres & Toltec Scenic Railroad is the nation's longest and oldest narrow-gauge railroad that makes it unique. Nor is it the fact that the passenger train climbs more than 3,000 feet during a 64-mile round-trip from here to Antonito, Colorado. What elevates it to curiosity status is the ownership.

The railroad was started in 1880 to haul silver, livestock, and timber out of the mountainous region. It also carried passengers until 1951 and then ceased operations entirely in 1967. But it was only a three-year shutdown. By 1970, with the help of railroad enthusiasts, the States of New Mexico and Colorado bought the land and agreed to run the line through a bi-state commission. That makes it the nation's longest and oldest narrow-gauge railroad that is owned and operated by two states. And as sort of a tribute to the two-state ownership, the train crosses the New Mexico–Colorado border eleven times on every trip between Chama and Antonito.

The railroad carries only passengers now and offers a variety of packages. One of the more popular leaves Chama at 10 a.m. and arrives at the end of the line in Antonito at 2:30 p.m. Those who go that route must either take a motor coach back to Chama or spend the night in Antonito, then catch the morning train back to Chama. Or vice versa.

Other offerings include round-trip excursions to such exotic stations as Osier and Cumbres over mountain passes and through deep gorges. Those who board in Chama will readily discover that many business places in town have railroad names like Chama Station Inn, the Parlor Car B&B, and the Gandy Dancer B&B. Something not quite so obvious is that Chama is derived from the ancient Tewa Pueblo word *tzama*, colorfully translated as "here they have wrestled."

Railroad buffs, wrestlers, and old brakemen alike can get more information at www.cumbrestoltec.com or by calling (888) CUMBRES (286-2737).

One Long, Straight Line
Cochiti Pueblo

The paved road between Cochiti Pueblo and Cochiti Lake wanders through a landscape that features undulations, hills, lesser mountains, and valleys. The muted browns and tans are pretty standard on both sides of the road, so there's nothing to make this stretch any more memorable than the thousands of miles of highway that cross the state.

Until, that is, the roadway levels out and there's the Black Line. That's not an official name; it's just what it looks like. And because it's so out of place—a solid straight line stretching across a tableau dominated by curves and swoops and dips—it looks like some giant used a ruler and felt-tip pen to connect Point A to Point B as on opposite sides of the horizon and then filled in the space below with dark scribbling.

But actually, it's nothing so romantic. The black line is Cochiti Dam, an earthen fill that is the twenty-third largest dam in the world by volume of material (62,849,000 cubic yards) used to create it. It's also one of the ten largest such dams in the United States and the eleventh largest dam of its kind in the world. The dam stretches for 8.8 miles, rises to a height of 251 feet, and measures 1,760 feet at the base as it impounds the Rio Grande. It's one of the four Army Corps of Engineers projects for flood and sediment control on the Rio Grande system. Construction began in 1965 and was completed in 1973 at a cost of $94.4 million.

The dam forms Cochiti Lake, a recreational body of water with a storage capacity of 50,000 acre-feet. It is stocked with smallmouth bass and northern pike and is a no-wake lake so boats are restricted to trolling speeds.

Cochiti Pueblo Indians opposed the dam because they lost a huge area of agricultural land as a result of construction and inundation. They filed a lawsuit against the Army Corps of Engineers that resulted in a public apology from the corps. The dam, however, remains.

And it still looks like a straight black line drawn by someone with limited imagination located off I-25 between Albuquerque and Santa Fe. Take exit 259 and travel north for about 11 miles.

The Fine Art of Mudding
Corrales

New Mexico is one of the select places on the planet where mudding is a team sport. It's because there are so many adobe buildings across the state and frequently (in general once a year), they have to be mudded, or more correctly, since it happens quite often, re-mudded.

Mudding is an art that has been practiced ever since humans learned how to make structures with adobe bricks. Because the bricks are essentially mud, they have to be re-mudded so they don't wash away when it rains. But because average annual rainfall in most of New Mexico is rather limited, the buildings hold up well, provided they get regular muddings.

Casa San Ysidro in Corrales is one such target of mudding crews. The old house, now a part of the Albuquerque Museum, hosts *Dia de Enjarrar* (Mudding Day) once a year. More than thirty volunteers show up for the event, during which they learn how to mix and apply the adobe mud. For the most part it's done the same way people have been doing it for centuries. They do, however, make one concession to mechanization by using a heavy-duty electric mixer to make the mud. The recipe is quite simple:

25 shovels full of dirt
15 shovels full of sand
2 handsful of hay, crumbled to an inch or two in length
about 5 ounces of bonding adhesive, if necessary
enough water to mix it smooth and thick

Once mixed, scoop the mud into buckets and use a special trowel when applying it to the existing surface that has been sprayed with water so it bonds with the new mud. If the mix is good, the mud adheres perfectly. A bad batch, however, won't be compatible and big chunks will fall off. Let dry. Repeat again next year.

Casa San Ysidro is located at 973 Old Church Road in Corrales. Take exit 233 off I-25 and go west on Alameda Boulevard, and then cross the Rio Grande and turn north on Corrales Road. Volunteers interested in mud-application duty with a serious overtone can get more information and tour times by calling (505) 898-3915 or visiting www.cabq.gov/museum/history/casatour.html.

Cooling Off in the Desert
El Malpais National Monument

So you're wandering around in the high desert and it's almost 100 degrees and you're overheated, and you're wishing there was a place where you could cool down while pondering a career move to the North Pole. You might consider spending some time in the Ice Cave.

It was formed back when things got really hot during a volcanic eruption. The volcano blew its stack, and when the lava runs, the outer layers cool, but a "river" of magma still runs through, until the eruption stops. When the magma drains away, it leaves a tube. The ice cave was formed when one of the tubes collapsed and filled with water that turned into ice.

Even today, it never melts. Even when it's unbearably hot outside, the temperature in the cave never rises above 31 degrees Fahrenheit. The floor is made of ice that is more than 20 feet thick and may be more than 1,300 years old. Early settlers used it as an early version of the refrigerator. And the layers of centuries-old frozen water still glisten a surreal blue-green when they reflect the filtered sunlight.

Ironically, the Ice Cave is right next door to Bandera Volcano, a crater that rose up "in volcanic fury" (according to the brochures) about 10,000 years ago. The contrasting combination of frigid cave and fiery volcano has given rise to the motto of "the Land of Fire and Ice," and the area is frequently referred to as "the most moon-like expanse of country on Earth."

Both the ice cave and volcano are privately owned and located on Highway 53 about 25 miles south of Grants. Take exit 81 (or 81A if coming from the west) off I-40 and head south on Highway 53 (aptly named Ice Caves Road) for 28 miles. For information and a map to the caves, log on to www.icecaves.com or call (888) ICE-CAVE (423-2283).

Spray-Paintless Graffiti
El Morro National Monument

Those who assume that graffiti is something that followed the invention of felt-tip markers and aerosol cans will be in for a delightful surprise if they ever visit the El Morro National Monument, where the names scrawled on the walls are hundreds of years old. And not only that, the works of these taggers are protected by the federal government, primarily because of their age.

While the rock formation now known as *el morro* ("the headland" in Spanish) goes far back into antiquity, the first recorded mention of the site occurred in 1583 when some Spanish soldiers stopped for water and noted it in their journals. For the next 300 years, hundreds of Spaniards passed the site

Centuries-old etchings mark some of the rocks at El Morro National Monument.

and many of them carved their names into the soft sandstone. Next came American soldiers, settlers, emigrants, freighters, and explorers, and many of them also left their marks.

The oldest, and most famous, example of this form of penmanship was hammered into the rock in 1605 by the first governor of New Mexico. He wrote (or chiseled): "Passed by here the Governor Don Juan de Oñate from the discovery of the Sea of the South on the 16th of April, 1605." That was fifteen years before the pilgrims landed at Plymouth Rock.

The brochure handed out at the visitor center gives this as a possible explanation for why people perform these defacing acts:

"Perhaps it was the notion of immortality—an inspiration for creative endeavors since the dawn of the human race—that compelled people to write their own lives into rock. Compared to our life spans, El Morro is timeless."

Anyone interested in seeing how they "decorated" before spray paint was invented can reach El Morro by driving south and then west for about 40 miles on Highway 53 out of Grants (off I-40, take exit 81 or 81A if you are going east). For details, log onto www.nps .gov/elmo or call (505) 783-4226.

Look! Up in the Sky! It's an Armada!
Farmington

On March 18, 1950, the banner headline on the front page of the *Farmington Daily Times* screamed: "Huge 'Saucer' Armada Jolts Farmington."

The subheads declared "Crafts Seen by Hundreds," "Speed Estimated at 1,000 MPH," and "Altitude 20,000 Feet," and the story began: "For the third consecutive day, flying saucers have been reported over Farmington . . ."

The witnesses quoted in the story all said they saw the objects before noon, highly unusual for UFO sightings. But, the report added, it was a windy day and a dust storm prevented clear vision. Despite

that, the paper noted, "Fully half the town's population is still certain today that they saw space ships or some strange aircraft—hundreds of them zooming through the sky yesterday."

People claimed there were as many as 500 of them, some as big as a bomber and traveling far beyond the speed of any earthly flying machine, real or imagined. An Air Force veteran told the reporter that if they were B-29 bombers, they had to have been traveling at 1,000 M.P.H., an unheard of speed at the time. Others said the craft appeared to be playing a game of high-altitude tag. But nobody reported vapor trails, engine noise, or shattered windows and the paper said, "In general Farmington accepted the phenomenon calmly, although it was reported that some women employees of a laundry became somewhat panicky."

Some said the objects were cotton balls, others claimed they were the fulfillment of a biblical prophecy, and opinion was divided between those who thought they were alien spaceships or some new aircraft designed by the federal government.

The newspaper's report noted that "whatever they were, they caused a major sensation in this community, which lies only 110 miles northwest of the huge Los Alamos Atomic installation." And the story also quoted residents who saw similar formations outside of Farmington about three hours later.

There has never been any official declaration about what occurred, and the *Times* never printed either a single follow-up or a retraction about the incident. But the topic remains hot in UFO-ology circles and the original newspaper story is still reproduced on many UFO-oriented Web sites.

Look! Up in the Sky! It's a Truck-sicle!
Farmington

The landscape along the main highway east of Farmington is relatively flat, an element that makes the truck-on-a-stick stand out. Or stick out.

A high-rise pickup truck gets
plenty of attention near Farmington.

★ ★

It's a 1928 Model A Ford truck perched atop a 50-foot steel tower in front of Moberg Welding, Inc. John Moberg, the owner, hoisted it up there in 2001 to attract attention. It works. It's visible for several miles in all directions, making it hard to miss even if you're not watching the skies for UFOs.

The old truck had been sitting around the yard for years before Moberg welded it to the steel pipe and hired a crane operator to raise it skyward. He said it's just under the FAA height limit, so he didn't have to install a strobe light to warn low-flying aircraft that there's a Model A in their flight pattern.

But some words of caution to those who drive by:

Look out while you're looking up. The shop is east of town at 5837 U.S. Highway 64 on the south side of the highway about ½ mile beyond the intersection of US 64 and Crouch Mesa Road/Highway 350.

The Quad-State Contortion Maneuver

Four Corners National Monument

Some tourists say they go to Four Corners National Monument because it's the only place in the nation where four states meet. Those who make that claim aren't being completely honest. The real reason they make the trip is to have their picture taken while standing in four states at the same time. And because of that, it's also a paradise for photographers who like to take pictures of people contorting themselves into weird shapes while smiling at the camera and saying "Cheese."

The four states meet at the intersection of a large X traced into a concrete slab. Through some strategic—but not necessarily graceful—placement of arms and legs, visitors can stand in New Mexico, Arizona, Colorado, and Utah at the same time. Those who manage to perform the maneuver will notice that weather conditions and scenery are pretty much the same in all four.

Several methods are used to achieve four-at-a-time positioning. The most common is the four-point squat, placing one foot and one hand in each quadrant. More adventuresome state counters will also employ the quad-state plop, a technique in which they simply flop down over the "X" and wave their arms and legs like a kid making a snow angel. Others go through gyrations that vaguely resemble dancing at a singles club, or somebody doing a bad impersonation of a four-legged tarantula.

The monument is located on U.S. Highway 160 in the far northwestern corner of New Mexico.

And the far northeastern corner of Arizona.

And the far southeastern corner of Utah.

And the far southwestern corner of Colorado.

There's an entry fee but it's well worth it for those who like to watch people pretzelize themselves. For more information, log on to www.mesaverde.com/fcmonument.htm.

Can You See Me Now?
Gallup

It's only natural, of course, that a store selling eyeglasses would incorporate eyeglasses into its signage. And so it is with Perfect Vision, which peddles reading glasses, look-good glasses, trendy eye wear, and glasses that protect vision from the harsh rays of the sun. What set the place apart from others is the sunglasses on the sign out front.

They're 10-footers, measuring across the front. The bows are equally huge. And they're also yellow, with orange-tinted lenses. They've been catching the eyes of passersby for about fifteen years. The huge cheaters were originally painted black. But, as one employee said, "yellow seems to attract more attention."

To make sure nobody misses this spectacle, the store has also erected three large plastic palm trees in the parking lot. Two are yellow; the other one's orange. Go see for yourselves. It's at 1109 North Highway 491. Take exit 20 off I-40, and head north. Perfect Vision will be on your left less than ½ mile up.

117

★ ★

The Key Word Here Is 'Big'

Gallup

Big pots. Big miner. Big murals. The world's biggest kachina. They're all works of art that line the streets of Gallup, and they're plenty big enough so they're sure to be noticed.

The city purchased the enormous Indian pots—ten of them—from a firm in Albuquerque and then commissioned local artists to adorn them with tribal symbols that represent area culture. They have been placed along freeway exits, on highway medians, and on downtown sidewalks. Each stands more than 6 feet tall so there's not much chance of accidentally walking into one nose first.

The oversized miner is made of boilerplate, so he has a rather lumpy and rusty complexion. Even though he stands more than 10 feet tall and weighs almost a ton, the miner struggles to pull an ore cart out of the ground in a small park on Montoya Boulevard.

The huge kachina, a representation of a beneficial Hopi Spirit, is a metal 20-footer painted yellow and stands across the street from the miner in Miyamura State Park. He's been greeting visitors for more than forty years, but not always from his present location. In an earlier time he stood along Route 66 as it passed through Gallup, but when I-40 usurped the old highway, the kachina was destined for the scrap heap until the city fathers decided to move him to the park.

Gallup calls itself "the city of murals" because of the many giant postcard like paintings that adorn downtown buildings. The tradition started with the WPA murals of the 1930s and was continued in 2004 when the city passed an initiative to create several new ones. Now, city officials declare Gallup has more WPA murals than any other city in New Mexico. To make sure you don't miss any, stop at the visitor center, 106 West Historic Highway 66, and ask for a map. Take exit 22 off I-40 and go south to Historic Highway 66. Turn right and go about ½ mile.

★ ★

And Now, Something Really Big
Gallup

Paso por Aqui is a sculpture that has been the object of wonder for millions of passersby who have seen it as they whistle through Gallup in either direction on I-40. But few stop to ask questions and even fewer take the time to have a closer look. For those unfortunates, here are some answers: It means "pass through here" and it's a tribute to the many groups of people that played roles in the city's history—Native Americans, miners, railroaders, ranchers, settlers, and all the others. Although it looks like a 30-foot circle from the freeway, it's actually a loop because the ends never meet to form a complete circle. One end emerges from the base to represent those who first came here, and the other end is a replica of a single railroad track.

Pasa Por Aqui rises above Gallup
and acts like a landmark.

★ ★

Charles Mallery and Robert Hymer, the artists, were hired by the Cultural Corridors Public Art on Scenic Highways Commission to create the big arch. Or circle. Or loop. Regardless of what it is, the sculpture is on Maloney Avenue between Pueblo and Grandview.

And Now, Some Little Things
Gallup

A few things that give Gallup a delightfully quirky edge:

- Miss that lonesome wail of a passing freight train? A total of 141 trains pass through the heart of the city every day. Not one of them stops.

- Although it's no longer a main highway, the city has not forgotten about Route 66. It is the single east-west thoroughfare through Gallup's 14-mile city limits, and every other local street either crosses it or dead-ends on it.

- Before he became a jelly-bean eating president, Ronald Reagan portrayed Notre Dame Football legend George Gipp in the 1940 film *Knute Rockne—All American.* Reagan also stayed in the El Rancho Hotel here (1000 East Highway 66). Now the hotel's restaurant features a burger called "the Ronald Reagan" and urges patrons to "eat one for the Gipper." The burger comes with bacon, cheese, and a side order of jelly beans.

- Local merchants claim that 85 percent of the entire world's trade in Native American arts and crafts are distributed through Gallup area businesses.

- Despite passage of the Indian Arts and Crafts Act in 1990, counterfeit Native American products are still a problem. It's a risky business, however. The penalties are stiff, including prison time for individuals and fines of up to $1 million for businesses.

Where to Catch a Really Big Dream

Grants

In Native American legends a dreamcatcher uses its webs to snare bad dreams. In Grants what may be the world's largest dream catcher is used to snare tourists.

Normal dream catchers are small, usually less than 8 inches in diameter, and the webs are string or yarn. But the one that sits in front of a gift shop here is closer to 8 feet across, and the web is made of ½-inch rope. A regulation dream catcher usually has a small feather attached to one side. This larger version also has a feather, but it's tin and about 4 feet long.

It went up in 2006 but apparently it didn't work very well, assuming that the owners of the gift shop had big dreams about striking it rich. The store closed in early 2007 and remains vacant. If, however, you have a big dream that needs to be captured, the device is on Santa Fe Avenue north of I-40 and next door to the Days Inn. Take exit 85 and head north. The dream catcher will be on your right.

Since it takes only a few minutes to thoroughly examine a giant dreamcatcher, and as long as you're in Grants looking for things of an unusual nature anyway, a visit to the only uranium mining museum in the world becomes a good way to fill some time.

The New Mexico Mining Museum at 100 North Iron Avenue isn't hard to spot because of the huge piece of mining equipment sitting out in front. Once inside, visitors can wander through a re-created uranium mine by taking a brief ride in a modern elevator dubbed "the Cage." It doesn't actually go underground, however; it just shakes and rattles a little so it feels like a journey to the depths.

The museum also displays pottery, tools, weapons and other arti-facts from the different cultures that have inhabited the area, dating back as far as A.D. 700. And, as an added bonus, guests will also learn that *el malpais* as applied to the nearby El Malpais National

★ ★

Conservation Area (site of the longest lava tube in the continental United States) came from the Spanish and translates into "the badlands."

For hours, fees, and other information, call (800) 748-2142.

Making Sure Nobody Gets Lost
Grants

Route 66 once stretched from Chicago to Los Angeles and was heralded in song, in the movies and on television. But today the fabled Mother Road has been reduced to small stretches of pavement in relatively isolated areas. Despite that, travelers from many nations follow the old trail on a hit-or-miss basis, often not sure if they're on the right road.

Now the Celebrate Route 66 Program should help them find their way. Inaugurated in 2006, the venture traces the route by painting large stencils on some of the remaining segments of the road as it passes through the cities and towns that once relied on it to bring trade and commerce. Sixty-six of the 4-by-6-foot stencils were applied in 30 locations between Mesita and the Arizona border. The first one was placed in front of the Grants City Hall. Convict crews painted the others in such places as Budville, Cubero, San Fidel, McCartys, Milan, and Bluewater Village.

The project began with the use of hand-wielded paint brushes but was completed with sprayers. The stencils were sprayed with black-and-white traffic paint garnished with glass beads for reflective power to make sure they're visible day and night.

The longest, still-existing section of the original highway in New Mexico runs through Cibola and McKinley counties. Santa Fe Avenue is Route 66 through Grants and Milan. Several vintage diners, a theater and a couple of classic motels still switch on their neon signs in the evening as a reminder of how things used to be. In other areas along the way, abandoned motels and gas stations are signs that those times are gone.

The program has an added benefit—drivers looking for the stencils are more likely to keep their eyes on the road. Of course, that benefit also has a drawback—drivers looking for stencils on the road might not see that eighteen-wheeler headed toward them.

If you don't know quite what to look for, you can see the stencil at 600 West Santa Fe Avenue in Grants. Just take exit 81 (or 81B if you are coming from the west) and go about ½ mile to the city hall, on your left.

A Second That Lasts Forever

Hernandez

It was toward dusk on October 31, 1941, and photographer Ansel Adams was driving along U.S. Highway 84 when he spotted what he considered an ideal photo op—darkening skies, a full moon, white crosses in a cemetery, a little white church, and clouds. Adams screeched his car to a stop and hauled his camera to a nearby hilltop and then began yelling at his assistants to bring more of his equipment. They couldn't find his exposure meter, which was invaluable because his large camera didn't have one built in, but he figured out the moon's luminescence and quickly took the shot.

One single photo.

He wanted to take another but the sun moved faster than he did, and the moment was gone. However, the one image he did capture has taken on a life of its own. It eventually became entitled "Moonlight, Hernandez, New Mexico, 1941."

The artist said later that it was "certainly my most popular image" because it "combined serendipity and immediate technical recall." Later, he added that "serendipity is just another word for lucky chance." Adams made several prints from the single negative, and sold them for as little as $50.

But that was only the beginning.

Today, the photo is a classic. It has appeared on more than two million posters and prints made from the original negative still sell for more between $50,000 and $70,000. In 1981, a print brought $71,500. In 2006, an original print brought a whopping $606,600 at a Sotheby's auction in New York.

The San Jose Catholic Church that appears in the photo is still there, but a newer, larger church has been erected nearby. They're both just off US 84 between mileposts 194 and 195. Hernandez is located where US 84 and Highway 74 intersect, about 5 miles north of Espanola.

So . . . Are the Hogback Suburbs Called Piggybacks?
Hogback

Even if you examine a map of New Mexico under a microscope, you won't find a town named Hogback because it's more of a formation than a town. Besides that, there's not much there, just a trading post, a convenience store, a laundry, and a church. It's hard to miss Hogback, however, due to the looming presence that gives the place its name.

It's a big lump of sandstone rising mightily out of the ground, part of a geological formation that runs from Canada to Mexico. Pieces of the formation pop up above the Earth's surface in New Mexico, Colorado, Montana, and Canada, but most of it is underground, sort of like that monster that supposedly swims around in Loch Ness. It has been called a hogback since the late 1800s, when the first Anglo settlers arrived and decided it needed a name. Then those who came later figured it was an appropriate designation, so they named everything else Hogback: the Hogback Trading Post, Hogback Grocery Store, Hogback Laundry, and Hogback Church of Christ.

The place with the romantic name is on US 64, just a couple miles west of Waterflow. And for those who insist on being technical, Hogback is actually part of Waterflow.

It's worth a stop because of the trading post that has been sitting on the same spot for more than 125 years. Founded by Joseph Wheeler in 1871, it has the distinction of being the oldest trading

A huge chunk of stone rising from
the ground gives Hogback its name.

post still operated by the same family. Over the years, it has also
served as a bank, mercantile store, and livestock brokerage institution. Current owner Tom Wheeler maintains a plentiful collection
of traditional and modern Navajo rugs, paintings, silver jewelry, and
alabaster art in a hogan-shaped building that contains 10,000 square
feet of display area.

The address is 3221 Highway 64 and you can usually talk with a
member of the founding family by calling either (505) 598-5154 or
(505) 598-9243.

A Stone Encampment

Kasha-Katuwe Tent Rocks National Monument

It is not uncommon for first-time visitors to look at the rock formations here and make clever deductions like "That must have

★ ★

been *some* powwow!" Or like "Did rock people live in those rock tents?"

They are uneducated, tongue-in-cheek observations, but somewhat understandable. The rocks that give the place its Anglo name are shaped like giant tepees that were pitched and then left out in the sun too long so they turned gray and got rock hard. None of this has anything to do with reality, of course.

The cone-shaped hoodoos are the products of volcanic eruptions that occurred more than six million years ago and left pumice, ash, and tuff deposits more than 1,000 feet thick. None of them is hollow, ruling out the possibility that this was once the site of an enormous encampment of tent dwellers. Some of the formations are topped by boulder caps that protect them against erosion. Others have lost their lids and are now being eaten away by the elements, although not fast enough so anybody's going to notice.

The name *Kasha-Katuwe* comes from the traditional Keresan language of the Cochiti Pueblo that surrounds the monument. It means "white cliffs,"

Strange rock formations look like they were abandoned by stone campers.

a logical designation because the tent rocks are located in front of some massive whitish bluffs. They're not pure white, but they're close enough.

The monument, located on the Pajarito Plateau, is considered a remarkable outdoor laboratory where sites reflecting human occupation spanning 4,000 years have been uncovered. During the 14th and 15th centuries, several large pueblos were established here and the descendants of the builders still inhabit the surrounding area, known as the Pueblo de Cochiti.

Campers who want to experience rock-hard accommodations can reach the monument by taking Highway 22 off I-25 at exit 259 and then following it to Cochiti Pueblo, where a right turn leads to the entrance.

Recycling Big-Time
Kirtland

So you think *you* got a lot of junk lying around in *your* backyard? Wait till you see this place. It's acre after acre after acre of throwaways, discards and stuff once considered worthless but now a hot item on the international market.

Valley Scrap Metal is what it's called and recycling scrap is what it does. The firm sits on ten acres but it looks larger than that because the assortment of scrap follows the contours of the landscape so it appears to wander over the hills and through the valleys and stretch clear up to the skyline. The major portion of this seemingly endless acreage is covered with junked cars, beer and soda cans, iron bars, steel pipes, and aluminum tanks. In all there's an estimated two million tons of used metal piled in scrap heaps that reach heights well over 25 feet and seem to go on forever.

And every day, huge machines grind, shred, cut, slash, and shear the metal into manageable chunks so it can be baled and trucked off for resale and recycling. Due to increasing demand from foreign

★ ★

countries, much of the salvage is shipped overseas. Most of the recyclables come from area residents, business places, and the mines, which bring in everything from garden tools to tire rims to pickup trucks that didn't hold up too well during head-on collisions.

Many of the bales are composed of crushed aluminum cans. Each bale is an 8-foot-by-8-foot cube, and each cube weighs 2,500 pounds. It takes 250 cans to make one pound. That means there are 625,000 crushed cans in each bale. No wonder the breweries and soft drink companies can afford those ads during the Super Bowl telecasts.

The firm is on the north side of US 64 as it passes through downtown Kirtland, about 4 miles east of Farmington. The phone number is (505) 598-5288.

The Most Unusual of the Unusual

Los Alamos

The business cards for the Black Hole call it "an unusual place." This is an understatement. It's more than unusual; it's probably the only one of its kind anywhere in the world. And besides that, the owner is a one-of-a-kind man determined to prevent the world from self-destructing.

Ed Grothus, the proprietor, worked at the Los Alamos National Laboratory from 1949 through 1969. It's the same place that earned a permanent spot in infamy as home to the Manhattan Project, which developed the first atomic bombs. Since leaving the lab, his life has been spent advocating peace and trying to bring an end to the manufacture of nuclear weapons.

As part of that campaign, Grothus commissioned Chinese artisans to create two granite obelisks that express his feelings about war and other harmful acts. Each stands more than 50 feet high and weighs more than twenty-two tons. Antinuclear inscriptions in fifteen different languages have been carved around each base. One says, "One bomb is too many." Another reads, "No one is secure unless everyone is secure."

Ed Grothus turns bomb casings into artwork
at his store in Los Alamos.

The huge pillars now sit in boxcar-sized shipping containers on his property while Grothus looks for a suitable spot to put them. He offered them to the Los Alamos County Art in Public Places advisory board but was turned down because, he said, "they didn't consider me an artist." Ironically, in September of 2007, Grothus received the Allan Houser Memorial Award, one of New Mexico's most distinguished artistic honors.

When he isn't campaigning to stop the proliferation of nuclear arms, Grothus operates the Black Hole, a unique surplus store and museum. He buys much of his inventory from the National Laboratory during regular auctions and then resells non-dangerous items to the public. His stock includes everything from desks, chairs, and file cabinets to devices that were once used to help make weapons of mass destruction but have been declared obsolete, like timers and triggers. He puts some things up for sale, stashes others in his museum, and converts a few into art. One of his works is a giant sunflower created from empty bomb casings.

Although he turned eighty-five in 2008, Grothus refuses to slow down and word of his efforts is spreading. He was the subject of a nine-page feature in the April 2006 edition of *Esquire* magazine, and he gleefully points out that Walter Cronkite got only two pages in the same issue.

His Black Hole is at 4015 Arkansas, where Highway 502 passes by the Los Alamos Medical Center; continue on Diamond Drive north through town for about 1 mile. Arkansas Avenue goes off to the left across from Thirty-Eighth Street. The phone is (505) 662-5053.

Doubling Up at the Old Waterhole
Los Alamos

Ashley Pond, which began as a natural pond, became one of this city's major attractions because of its pleasant surroundings. It's located close to the heart of downtown and is enhanced by a number of sculptures that are part of the Los Alamos County art collection.

Many years ago, blocks of ice were removed from the pond during the winter and stored in the icehouse that once stood nearby, and schoolchildren used the icehouse as an arena for both summer and winter sports.

The pond is named after the founder of the Los Alamos Ranch School, and his students couldn't pass up the opportunity to create a sort of word overkill because his name was Ashley Pond. So technically, that makes the pond's official name the Ashley Pond Pond.

Ashley Pond is midway between the Los Alamos Medical Center and the Los Alamos County Airport on Highway 502.

★ ★

A House of Pancakes and Prayer

Los Alamos

There's something just a tiny bit unsettling about eating in the La Vista Restaurant in the Best Western Hilltop House Hotel here. Once you know its military and religious backgrounds, you get this sense that you have to be on your best behavior—or else. This probably stems from the fact that the restaurant used to be a church and it sits on a former military installation.

When Robert Waterman decided to build the Hilltop House back in the 1990s, he first purchased a vacant lot where an Army motor pool once stood in downtown Los Alamos. Then he bought a chapel from a military base in Lubbock, Texas, and had it taken apart, piece by piece. His crews marked each individual piece and trucked them to Los Alamos, where they were reassembled as part of his hotel.

The former chapel now seats ninety customers and features floor-to-ceiling stained glass windows surrounded by clear glass on the east end. The pews and pulpit are gone, but the beams that grace-fully arch across the interior are intact. The choir loft is now used for banquets. Diners also get a view of the nearby Sangre de Cristo Mountains that is doubly gorgeous when the sun rises over them in the morning.

The hotel is at 400 Trinity Drive, right on the corner of Trinity Drive and Central Avenue, a little over ½ mile east of Ashley Pond. The restaurant is on the third floor. For reservations call (800) 462-0936.

You don't have to say grace before the meal but it probably wouldn't hurt, all things considered.

A Stone of Mystery

Los Lunas

The Mystery Rock is part of a basalt column that toppled over a long, long time ago in a valley below what is now called Hidden Mountain, about 18 miles south of Los Lunas. What makes it a mystery are the

214 letters carved into its surface. They have been examined, reexamined, translated, photographed, studied, pored over, and deciphered for almost 200 years.

During that time the letters—and the words they form—were labeled Navajo, Mormon, Greek, Hebrew, Russian Cyrillic, Etruscan, Egyptian, and a hoax. Those who studied them came up with a variety of conclusions, including one observation that students from the University of New Mexico had carved the letters as a prank. A Harvard scientist has proposed that the stone is a Hebrew Decalogue, the Ten Commandments. But others said it was a different version of the Ten Commandments and that conclusion was hailed as the correct one until the 1970s, when an Albuquerque woman claimed it was written by Zakyneros, a Greek scholar who wrote in both ancient Phoenician and early Greek around 500 B.C.

The actual age may never be determined because clean-up work at the site over the years has destroyed any possibility of using modern dating techniques. But one test that compared the inscription to that of a nearby petroglyph dates the stone between 500 and 2,000 years old. Critics scoff at that analysis, saying that the 1,500-year gap proves the method of testing is inaccurate.

The stone is easier to read today, however, because Boy Scouts have regularly gone to the site and traced the letter outlines in chalk.

Linguists and thrill seekers who want to try their hand at answering the unanswered can still get to the rock but it's a difficult journey. It's located on land belonging to the Isleta Pueblo, so a permit from the State Land Grant office in Albuquerque is an absolute necessity. Those who go there without a permit can be arrested. But if you simply *have* to go, call the Land Grant office at (505) 841-8705 for information.

A Growling Rah-Rah-Rah
Los Lunas

Water-tank art isn't exactly common in New Mexico, but several examples of creativity are painted on the storage units. One of the

★ ★

best is here, where a huge city water tank is adorned with two snarling tigers.

There's a tiger on the east side and another on the west and all the space in between is filled with orange and black stripes, which is the way a tiger-ed water tank should look. The big felines were painted by Robert Vialpando, a local sign painter and a member of the city council. He created them to honor the athletes at nearby Los Lunas High School because the school mascot is the tiger. The tank is very visible from I-25 on the north edge of the city, about ½ mile north of exit 203.

The Los Lunas High School Tigers show up on both sides of a city water storage tank.

Chugging Some Ale

Los Lunas

Anyone who has ever plowed a field on a hot summer day will instantly recognize the definite connection between tractors and cold beer. But that premise gets carried to the extreme at the Tractor Brewing Company, where big mechanical chuggers coexist with human chug-a-luggers on a daily basis.

The brewery, also known as the Beer Farm, produces a wide variety of potables that are sold in the adjacent restaurant. They carry farmy names like Farmers Tan Red Ale, Sodbuster Pale Ale, Haymaker Honey Wheat, and Double Plow Oatmeal Stout, plus Inebriator, Farmers Daughter Red Ale, Munich Dunkel, Bumper Crop, and Half-Acre Hefe-Weizen.

And the tractor theme is everywhere. The parking area showcases restored John Deeres, Massey Fergusons, and Farmalls mixed in with some Allis Chalmers equipment, plus plows, hay rakes, and other farming necessities. The roof over the tasting area resembles a barn and two minitractors have taken up residency on a gate. The brew house is in the rear of the main building and once the brewing process is complete, the spent grains are whisked away by area farmers who use it as cattle feed.

Toy tractors abound inside the complex. They're everywhere—in the windows, on the walls, mounted on a miniature Ferris wheel and carousel. There's even a farm reference in the company's Web address—www.getplowed.com. The place is also an eatery and diners can look out the windows and gaze across the surrounding farmlands at the nearby Manzano Mountains.

The company opened in October 1999 and its beers have been getting favorable reviews, including one that noted the Double Plow Stout is "not excessively roasted or chocolaty." Those who want to feel their oats while they're ingesting some will find the brewery at 120 Nelson Lane, where the phone number is (505) 866-0477. Take exit 203 off I-25 and go east on Highway 6 for about 2 miles. At the fork, go left onto Main Southeast and take your first right onto Lujan Road.

An Artsy Sort of Place
Madrid

It doesn't take long to realize that this small town isn't like other small towns. Those who stop will find that out in a hurry if they utter

★ ★

something like "Madrid is a very nice place," and one of the locals corrects them on the pronunciation. It's "MAD-rid," not "Ma-DRID" like that place in Spain.

Also, there's the décor. The streets of Madrid are lined with the work of local artisans and every one of their works is a departure from what most would consider the norm. They're a bit hard to describe because they go beyond unusual, way past way out, further out than far out.

For example, there's a sculpture that resembles the drawing of an atom, but it's made of large string balls and steel poles. Across the street, an 8-foot tin musician strums a guitar, and just down the road, an archway composed of huge plaster chiles sits in somebody's front yard.

Continuing the curious theme, a concrete 3-foot foot sits in front of a store while a fence made of mattress springs keeps the unwanted out of somebody's front yard. An image of the sun has eyes that formerly served as ceiling speakers. And the main street also features a ceramic totem pole, a sculpture of car fenders, a face carved in lava rock, and a shop made of driftwood. Oddity lovers will also find a store located in what used to be a railroad boxcar. And a purple house adorned with large painted-on sunflowers.

The current population stays around 300, but Madrid was the center of all coal mining in the area and had thousands of inhabitants back in the late 1800s and early 1900s, when the annual Christmas display included 150,000 lights. The miners dug coal from the surrounding Ortiz Mountains but the mines closed in the 1950s and Madrid became a near-ghost town. In the 1970s, area artists began moving in and partially resurrected the place. The town was also used as a location during the filming the 2007 movie Wild Hogs.

Art lovers and curiosity seekers alike can find Madrid 17 miles south of Santa Fe on Highway 14, also known as the Scenic Turquoise Trail.

Immortalized Geezers
Madrid

Suppose you're in Madrid and somebody sidles up to you and goes, "Pssst, you wanna buy some pictures of naked people?" Beware of the offer. The naked people are all geezers who have been around for more than six decades.

There are thirteen of them, blatantly posing in the same amount of clothing they were wearing when they came into this world, just so they could get their pictures on a calendar; one for each month and one for the cover. They shed their boots and blue jeans to appear sans clothing on a month-by-month work titled "Nude Geezers 2008." The crusty models include a veteran fighter pilot, a doctor, an impresario, a retired stockbroker, a cowboy, even the photographer who came up with the idea. And they're all, in the words of one, "nakeder'n a freshborn."

As Len Self, one of the models, put it, "All clothes does is cover up beauty." But beauty in this case includes some anatomy that probably shouldn't be exposed (as it were) to the populace.

Of course, it's not porno naked. Cowboy hats, sculpture, a saddle, and other items cover the no-no parts so the calendars can be offered to the general public, not just to people wearing trench coats, fake eyeglasses, and false noses. There are, however, a couple of bare (but surprisingly wrinkle-free) sixty-plus bottoms.

The calendar was the brainchild of area photographer Doug Wesley, also one of the models, who said he did it as a sixtieth birthday present to himself. Wesley and his calendar boys provided the finances and they all showed up to autograph the calendars at a Nude Geezer Weenie Roast in September 2007.

Whether they'll do it again for 2009 depends on how many of the 2008 version they sell. For more information on where to buy an over-the-hill calendar featuring over-the-hill nudes, log on to http://shop.geezers-illustrated.com.

A Place of Her Own

Madrillos

Madrillos isn't shown on any New Mexican road maps, which is understandable because it isn't a real place. Surreal, maybe, but not really real. It's one of those "beauty is in the eye of the beholder" creations, and in this particular case, the beholder better have a good sense of quirkiness.

More commonly known as either Tiny Town or Bone Town, the collection of bones, discarded car parts, immobilized mannequins, old signs, flags, jewelry, and curious paint jobs is an ongoing artwork being executed by Tammy Lange, who prefers to be called Tattoo Tammy or Tatt-II Tammy.

Her assortment of artifacts includes a human skeleton riding a skeleton motorcycle, the legs of a plastic dummy sticking out of a

Tattoo Tammy creates art to die for
on her spot of ground outside Madrid.

★ ★

bucket, signs that warn against hollering, weathered doll houses, tin cans, and skulls. In her ongoing quest for usable items, she scours the countryside and accepts donations from people she calls "boners." She explains that "anyone can be a boner; they just have to make a bone-ation."

She's called Tattoo Tammy because she is covered with body art. And she calls her place Madrillos because it needed a name and Madrillos was better than what some of the neighbors call it—the Eyesore. But she laughs it off and talks about her plans to publish a magazine called *Better Bones and Gardens*.

"This is where art dies to live," she explains with a chuckle. "It's my dream. My vision. My therapy."

Madrillos, or Tiny Town, or Bone Town, or whatever you want to call it is on the west side of Highway 14, two miles north of Madrid. There's no phone, no website, no fax. Just a bunch of bones.

A Place for Rugs
Newcomb

The name of the Historic Toadlena Trading Post and Weaving Museum takes up almost as much space as the museum itself. And even though it's rather isolated, the place is amazing and its impact is enormous because it serves as the area's largest employer while preserving an almost-lost art.

The museum is small, undoubtedly among the smallest in the world. It takes up about a third of the trading post's interior, and it's only ten years old. But it houses one of the world's finest collections of Navajo rugs, all created by weavers from the immediate area. They hang in exhibits that can take as little as five minutes or as long as hours to go through, depending upon the viewer's interest in the craft.

The collection has been gathered by Mark Winter, who bought the trading post in 1997, gutted it, and restored it to its original 1906 condition. So it features a potbellied stove, a barber's chair, vintage wooden display cases, and an old-time photo album containing pictures of every rug Winter ever purchased. Then he converted a portion of the building into the museum to display some of the rugs. They range from large works created by the old master weavers to tiny rugs the size of stove pads, the works of beginners just learning the skill.

When he bought the post, Winter was concerned that weaving was becoming a lost art. So he began paying top prices to encourage weavers but demanded that their rugs be made like they were in the old days, with natural dyes and wool they carded and spun themselves. Now the trading post is the major source of income for about 120 weavers, who keep credit accounts as advances in the form of money, good or services. They pay the advances off with their rugs.

And it still operates like the original trading posts did. Quite simply, Winter trades wool and groceries for rugs.

The trading post and museum are west of US 491, about halfway between Shiprock and Gallup, around Newcomb. Turn west off 491 at the Mustang Gas Station, then follow the signs for about 11 miles. It's a paved road except for the last quarter mile. There's no admission fee. For better directions and more information, log on to www.ToadlenaTradingPost.com or call (888) 420-0005.

A Skullful Woodworker
Placitas

Gene McClain builds furniture, chairs, mostly. He uses wood and stain. And skulls. Cow skulls, elk skulls, goat skulls. Whatever skulls he can find, as long as they're big enough. He ferrets them out at yard sales, antique shops, and roadside stalls. And if they're broken, as skulls often are, it doesn't matter. He'll fix them.

McClain, a retired high school teacher, builds the chairs in his studio, which is also his garage. He began creating skull chairs shortly after leaving the teaching profession because, he says, he wanted to become an artist but the competition was too stiff. So he turned to

★ ★

folk art. Or camp art. It doesn't make any difference to him what it's called. He also makes chairs that resemble motorcycles, Native Americans and movie stars, and three-legged stools using fence posts.

When creating a skull chair, he starts with a skull. If it's broken, he uses fiberglass to fill in the cracks, which is all right because he paints the skulls once he has them mounted on a chair, so nobody can tell the difference. Also, using broken skulls is more economical because complete skulls "get pretty darn expensive." For the wooden parts, he uses pine or spruce, which he stains or paints once the chair is complete but before the skull is attached.

Some of his finished products stand 7 feet tall, so the skulls, which are mounted on top of the chair back, get a good look at what's for dinner. Those who don't mind eating with something deceased watching over them will find McClain's work in his garage at 13 Las Huertas Road in Placitas and the Woodworkers and Friends Gallery at 8380 Cerrillos Road (exit 278 on I-25 and north on Highway 14 for ½ mile), in the Santa Fe Outlet Center. For more information, call him at (505) 771-0821 or send him an e-mail at gene_mcclain@comcast.net.

A Boy Who Never Quite Grew Up
Sandia Park

Ross Ward started carving miniatures during his boyhood and was still creating them before his death in 1998. The result of that dedication to a dream is Tinkertown Museum, a fantasy land of little folks, the Old West, circus scenes, musicians, and other stuff, most of them carved from scrap lumber and all of them done to scale.

According to his autobiography, titled *I Did All This While You Were Watching TV*, Ward's interest in small-scale things began after a visit to Knott's Berry Farm in California as a boy. He returned to his home in Aberdeen, South Dakota, and created a small town in his backyard. That one was leveled when the family moved, but Ward built others in between stints as a sign painter, circus hand, and army draftee. In 1968 he and his wife found a five-room cabin in the

Sandia Mountains, which he gradually filled with his carvings. They called his collection Tinkertown and took it on the road for a couple of years before converting the cabin into a museum that eventually became a twenty-four-room structure, each room filled with Ward's little people and little things.

Today, for a mere $3, visitors can watch animated musicians play a folk tune, watch a circus parade, and examine the walls Ward created with 50,000 bottles and tons of cement. They walk past old license plates used to cover uneven spots on the walls, step across horse-shoes embedded in the concrete, and have their futures foretold by a Gypsy encased in an old fortune-telling machine.

Since his death, Ward's family has taken over the operation, so they're in charge of thousands of carvings, musical instruments, ani-mals, buildings, streets, and boardwalks, all made of scrap materials, all done while everyone else was watching television.

Tinkertown is located on the Turquoise Trail at 121 Sandia Crest Road. From I-40, take exit 175 and travel 6 miles north on Highway 14 through Cedar Crest. Turn left on Highway 536, the road to San-dia Crest, and Tinkertown is 1.5 miles farther on the left. For more information, visit www.tinkertown.com, or call (505) 281-5233, and the keyword is fantasy.

A Fence Guarding Wide Open Spaces
Shiprock

The formation known both as *Tse'Bit'a'i* ("the rock with wings") and Shiprock Pinnacle attracts the attention from passersby and photog-raphers, and justifiably so. Shiprock by itself rises 1,700 feet above the desert floor along U.S. Highway 491, a factor that makes it visible from all the Four Corners states (New Mexico, Arizona, Colorado, and Utah), up to 100 miles away.

The Navajo people teach their young that the landmark is the site of their creation. They believe the towering formation is a ship that brought the ancestors of the *Dine* (Navajo people) to this land.

Another version springs from an ancient folk myth that says the rock was once a great bird that transported the ancestral people to their lands.

Those who want a closer look may do so by taking BIA Road 34 west off U.S. 491 for about 8 miles to what looks like a giant stone fence, also a spectacular natural phenomenon. It's about 10 feet thick at the base, stands about 40 feet high, and runs for more than 200 yards.

A natural first impression is that some giant sculptor hammered and whacked a big chunk of lava rock into the shape of an abstract fence and then just left it there. A more scientific explanation is that eons ago, lava flowed into a fissure and when the ground around it eroded away over the centuries, the fencelike formation was left standing. A dirt road leads past the lava fence all the way to Shiprock Pinnacle, but visitors should be aware that the big formation is sacred to the Navajo people so climbing is not allowed.

Travelers should also avoid using the dirt road after heavy rain because it turns into mud, muck, and ooze. There's not a tow truck anywhere in sight and because the area is so isolated and sparsely populated, cell phones don't work much of the time.

A Chairless Cafe
Shiprock

The Chat & Chew Cafe may not be the world's smallest eatery but it is most certainly among the leaders. The establishment has been a Shiprock institution for decades, but nobody ever sits around gabbing over a cup of coffee or fries because it's too small.

The building looks like a dollhouse with a steeply sloped roof and walls that slant inward. The exterior measurements are about 12 feet by 12 feet; it's even smaller inside so there's no room for such usual restaurant amenities as tables, chairs, menus, and napkin holders. In fact, there's barely room for the cook and the lone waitress. Customers walk in through the front door, take one step to reach the counter, and place their orders. Then they can either stand aside in front of the counter or wait outside for their food. And once they're served, they sit and dine outside at picnic benches or eat in their vehicles.

Despite that, the cafe is a popular place, particularly at noon when diners pull up, read the menu (posted outside because there's no room inside), get their munchies, and eat under the shade of a huge old cottonwood tree. The restaurant has been there since 1958; the tree was there a long time before that because it's so big it takes the outstretched arms of five people to encircle it.

The cafe is on the south side of Highway 516 on the east edge of Shiprock. The phone number is (505) 368-4875 but don't bother calling to reserve a table because there are no tables to reserve.

Stomping to Glory
Turley

In order to fully understand the process, picture this:

Teams of adult men and women jumping up and down on some helpless grapes, squishing them into a pulp in a wooden tub while the stereo plays grape-crushing music and a grape-crazed crowd urges them to mash those little grapies even harder.

This unusual behavior is called, logically, the Great Grape Stomp and it takes place in September as part of a fall festival sponsored by the Wines of San Juan, a local vineyard. The stompers form two-person teams and compete in a variety of categories, such as best costume, best technique, and most grape juice stomped. One team member is the stomper, whose role is obvious. The other is the swabbie, who collects the juice and skins.

(For those interested in procedural purity, the practice is also called "foot treading," which may be technically correct but lacks the verbal punch of "grape stomping.")

Stomping methods range from "the Lucy," patterned after an infamous *I Love Lucy* episode, to "the running man," a 1980s retro

★ ★

step popular among those who aren't afraid of slipping. Some use only one leg to stomp; some do the twist; some just hop. Regardless of technique, stompers say doing it by foot is better than mechanization because they can feel any clumps and break them up. The downside is that stomping is much slower and labor intensive, and stompers produce only about half as much must (grape juice) as machines.

Once all the stomped stuff has been gathered, it's placed into vats and goes through the procedure that will eventually turn it into wine. Those who fear they might catch athlete's foot from drinking the Chianti can relax. The acidity of the refining process destroys any unwanted substances. And to those who might abstain from the competition because they don't want permanently purple feet, be not afraid. Most varieties used here are non-stainers.

Grape smooshers and oenologists alike can visit the Wines of San Juan at 233 Highway 511, just west of Turley. Get more information by calling (505) 632-0879 or visiting www.winesofthesanjuan.com.

White among the Sorta-White Whites

White Rock

The rocks and canyons that gave this community its name were probably white eons ago, but now they're sort of a brownish white, the result of years of exposure to the elements. This does not alter the beauty of the surrounding area because the brownish white rocks are, despite the diffusion of color, still magnificently spectacular as they rise from the canyon floors like huge warships cruising across a desert sea.

White Rock Canyon was carved over the eons by the Rio Grande through basalt and tuff, and averages 1,000 feet deep. But its namesake traces its origins only back to 1947 when the United States Atomic Energy Commission bought the land from the Forest Service to build a temporary community for construction crews working at the Los Alamos National Laboratory. They named it White Rock, but it was abandoned in 1953 and all the buildings were gone by 1958. The current White Rock began in 1963 and is largely a bedroom community for employees at the lab.

One white rock lends credibility to the White Rock designation, however. It's sitting there on the corner and sometimes it's a brilliant white. But it's also an artificial white so it doesn't count. The boulder-size rock is more like a sign than a hunk of calcium carbonate because it gets a new paint job almost every day.

Teenagers do the artwork. They profess their true loves, team spirit, and political ambitions on the surface of the rock through use of spray paint and felt-tip markers. The base color is white so the new slogans and love notes leap out at the passerby because they're applied in various hues of red, green, and blue. Or any other color available at the time.

This example of youthful enthusiasm awaits its daily redecoration at a Conoco gas station on the corner of Rover Boulevard and Highway 4, about a block north of the visitor center. And because of the vital role it serves as a communicator, there's nothing illegal about a practice that other towns might view as graffiti.

White Rock is off Highway 4, about five miles south of the intersection with Highway 502 at a point six miles east of Los Alamos.

A Resting Place for Ol' Yeller
Zuni Pueblo

Most travelers who pass through this village stop and take photographs of the *he:bok'owe* (also known as hornos), beehive-shaped mud ovens that are still used to bake bread. Several of them are spread throughout the community. But others whip out their cameras when they come across the old yellow machine that has become at one with an elm tree.

The machine apparently started life a long time ago as a winch. It's the size of a small tractor and has cables and ran on a track, like an army tank, but no brand name or anything else indicates its

★ ★

origins. Nobody in the community seems to know how long it has been sitting in its current location, but even a novice botanist can readily assume that it's been quite a few years because of the elm tree. It's growing up through the machine.

The trunk of the elm has forced its way through the open spots on the machine and has reached a height of more than 30 feet. In some places the tree has wrapped itself around the steel bars and beams in such a way that elm and machine will never be separated without putting a real bad hurt on one or the other.

Fans of symbiotic relationships will find this unlikely combo just west of the A:ShiWi Tribal Headquarters. But always ask before taking a photo, just as a matter of courtesy.

The Pueblo of Zuni is considered to be the most traditional of the nineteen New Mexico pueblos, and further claims to have the highest concentration of skilled artisans on the North American continent. It's also the largest pueblo, covering the 45,000 acre reservation and unattached land holdings in other parts of New Mexico and Arizona.

The pueblo and the unlikely couple are on Highway 53, about 10 miles east of the Arizona-New Mexico border.

3

Southeast

Whenever I think of big history, big holes in the ground, and big football heroes, I can't help but think of southeastern New Mexico. The lore and legend of Billy the Kid and the fact and fancy of Roswell could make up their own curiosities books, and I devoted quite a bit of time seeking out information on both. But I also came across a good variety of items not related to gunfighters and aliens.

I toured a museum dedicated to an immortal fire-fighting bear and viewed the works of a relatively unknown artist (who also happens to be a bear). The people of this area train racing iguanas, build barbecues in the form of six-shooters and bulls, decorate donkeys, paint images of their favorite athlete on storefronts, and immortalize football teams on water storage tanks.

While wending my way through oil rigs that rise and fall like giant aphids, I met a man who collects windmills, another who organizes a golf tournament in a cow pasture, and a woman whose soft drink collection has taken over her restaurant. I bought a snack at a fast food stand located 750 feet beneath the surface of the earth and rode in a seventy-year-old elevator that mercifully still worked.

Through it all, the people of the southeast greeted me with warm hearts and open arms. They returned phone calls, kept appointments, directed me to the best watering holes, and gave me shelter at a reduced rate. Most importantly, not one of them threatened to call 911 when I asked if they had ever seen any little green men.

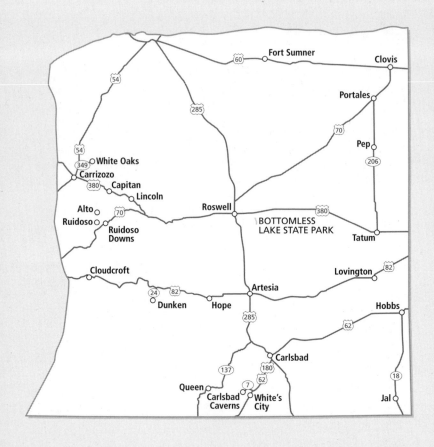

Southeast

Culture in the Pines

Alto

The Spencer Theater in itself is not all that unusual. It's large, draws some big-name entertainers, and offers a wide variety of attractions, ranging from Dave Brubeck to Crystal Gayle to the Russian National Ballet to the Smothers Brothers, Pam Tillis, and Chuck Mangione.

But what makes it a true curiosity is where it's located.

The address is 108 Spencer Road, Alto, New Mexico, or about 5 miles to the east of town on Highway 220. Alto has a population of around 800, which means that about 62 percent of the citizenry could fit into the 514-seat indoor theater, and even if everybody showed up, they wouldn't fill the 1,200-seat outdoor amphitheater. But although situated in what might be considered a remote mountain area, this first-class facility rises seven stories above a clearing in an otherwise forested landscape.

The building, made of 440 tons of mica-flecked Spanish limestone, was designed by New Mexican architect Antoine Predock to reflect a silhouette of the Sierra Blanca, a glacial peak that gazes down on the area. Predock also included a stepped fountain that resembles a mountain stream. Inside, four works of world-renowned glass artist Dale Chihuly give the theater additional sparkle to complement Predock's design.

The 50,000 square foot structure, built at a cost of $22 million, sits on top of 72 acres. The facility was funded by Dr. A. N. Spencer in memory of his wife, Jackie Spencer, a Dow Jones heiress who first visualized the theater in the pines to bring culture to places like Alto, Ruidoso, Carrizozo, Capitan, Nogal, and Glencoe.

For more information, log on to www.spencertheater.com or call (888) 818-7872.

Don't Mess with Them Dogs
Artesia

This city's huge water-storage tank has been painted to honor the Artesia High School Bulldogs and their dominance in football. The circular mural dominates the landscape west of the city, and depicts a mammoth bulldog surrounded by football helmets. Each helmet represents a state championship and the Bulldogs win so often that the décor has to be redone almost every other year.

Since 1957 the Bulldogs have won their division championship twenty-six times. That trophy accumulation includes five "three-peats" (1967–1969, 1974–1976, 1982–1984, 1992–1994, and 1996–1998) and a record of 454 wins against only 148 losses and 15 ties. Just to show all those others weren't chance happenings, the team also won the championship in 2007, exactly 50 years after this remarkable string began. The tank is at the east edge of town on U.S. Highway 82.

Ironically, no big-name college or professional football players have emerged from the program, but the school does boast that Edgar Mitchell is among its graduates. Mitchell became an astronaut and was the sixth man to walk on the moon, out of a total of twelve. He took the lunar stroll in 1971 as a member of the Apollo 14 crew.

And, as another indication of the high regard accorded the teams by the townspeople, the Town Clock at the corner of South Seventh Street and West Main includes the Bulldogs' fight song in its chiming repertoire.

Was She Intuitive or Just Lucky?
Artesia

One of the largest sculptures in New Mexico is *The Derrick Floor*, a bronze representation of a four-man crew working on a drilling rig that stands 34 feet tall. Artesia's artistic centerpiece, this work of art literally echoes the real derrick that rises above the Navajo Refining Company facility at the other end of Main Street.

The work is a bronze representation of the crew on a life-sized drilling rig that was cut off at the 34-foot mark. But, to display the importance of the men who worked on the rigs, artist Vic Payne made the crew members 125 percent life-size. The piece was dedicated in April 2004 "to the men and women who take the risks and do the work to find, produce and refine New Mexico oil and gas."

Two smaller sculptures share the small park with *The Derrick Floor*. One depicts a seated woman who is pointing to something. That something, history shows, was oil.

A sculpture of the woman who pointed to the oil is part of a bronze oil well scene in Artesia.

Her name was Mary Yates, and she earned a niche in local history back in 1924. Her husband, Martin, was part of an oil-drilling partnership that had sunk two unsuccessful wells. The partnership's geologist, dismayed at the two failures, wouldn't specify a third site so the selection fell on Martin Yates. But apparently, he didn't want the job either so he asked his wife to use her intuition and pick a spot. According to the inscription next to the sculpture, when they came to what felt like the right spot, she said, "Stop here." So they did, and they drilled and they struck it rich.

Since that time, the company founded by the Yateses has produced 3.9 billion barrels of oil and 20.9 trillion cubic feet of natural gas out of tens of thousands of wells.

The sculpture park is at the corner of South Sixth Street and West Main.

Ruminating with a Ruminant
Artesia

Among the items on display in the Artesia Visitors Center and Chamber of Commerce, located in the magnificently restored Santa Fe Railroad depot at 107 North First Street (also US 285), is a cow with a television set in her belly. Her name is Bessie. She's not a real cow. Real cows actually do put lots of things in their stomachs because

A cow with a television set in her tummy
tells a story in Artesia.

they are ruminants so they can chew their cuds as part of the digestive process but even with that advantage, TV sets are not in their normal diets.

Also, it's a one-channel TV set so those who go there and press the right button shouldn't expect to see such regular television fare as "Cow I Met Your Mother," "Cownanza" or "Holsteinfeld." Instead, they get to watch a video that relates the history of the dairy industry in the region. It's all part of the Pecos Valley Dairy Museum, also housed in the center. Inside the museum a digitized clock keeps track of how many gallons of milk have been produced since the first of the year.

Those who watch Bessie's tummy and take in the museum often refer to it as an "udderly moo-ving" experience.

Another Bad-Man Tribute
Artesia

New Mexicans seem to have a sense of forgiveness in their hearts for those who have done them wrong. The outlaw Billy the Kid is a legend all across the state. Down near the Mexican border, Columbus has erected a statue of Pancho Villa even though he once invaded their town. Up in Clayton, an entire section of a museum is dedicated to train robber Black Jack Ketchum. Over in a Cimarron hotel, there's a plaque that lists all the men bad guy Clay Allison gunned down.

And here in Artesia, they're creating a bronze memorial that pays tribute to the cattle rustler.

It's one of three monumental sculptures in "The Cattle Drive," a series that honors the development of the region's ranching industry. The first statue is Trail Boss, the owner of a small herd of cattle; the second is Vaquero, the cowboy who alerts the owner about the cattle thief. And the third will be Rustler, an outlaw who makes his living by stealing cows. It will be installed in 2009.

Although each one was created by a different artist, all three pieces are larger than life and are strategically placed in the

★ ★

downtown historical area in a two block stretch along Main Street, so they're all visible at the same time. They included the rustler because, according to literature distributed by the chamber of commerce, "he was part of our heritage."

For more information on art in the city, log on to www.artesia chamber.com or call (800) 658-6251.

Just the Bear Facts
Capitan

The story of how a little cub orphaned by a forest fire became a national celebrity is fairly well known. But, for those whose interests don't include fairy tale–like stories, here's a brief rundown:

He was a black bear cub rescued by firefighters after a human-caused fire burned 17,000 acres in the Lincoln National Forest in 1950. After rangers nursed him back to health, the cub was flown to Washington, D.C., where he lived in the National Zoo until his death in 1976. After they saved him, the rescuers named him Hotfoot. But it was later changed to Smokey Bear and he became the symbol of the forest-fire prevention campaign.

Smokey became so famous that he had his own zip code at the zoo because of the large amount of fan mail he received. He also was depicted on a postage stamp issued in 1984, the only time an individual animal has been so honored. Meanwhile, the folks back in Capitan formed the Smokey Bear Club and raised enough money to build a log cabin to serve as a museum for their favorite bear, even though he was living clear across the country. It's still there, filled with Smokey Bear memorabilia, right next to the Smokey Bear Histor-ical Park. And after he died, Smokey's remains were returned to New Mexico and buried in the national forest where his life started.

But what most bear fans don't know is how the "the" was added to his name. It happened in 1952 when Steven Nelson and Jack Rol-lins wrote "Smokey the Bear." In order to maintain the rhythm of the song, they added "the," which made sense musically but caused some lasting confusion over the correct name. Regardless of rhythm and meter, the name is, and has always been, Smokey Bear. So there.

The museum is at the intersection of U.S. Highway 380, Highway 240, and Highway 48. And here's another bit of lore that most don't realize—this Smokey Bear wasn't the original Smokey Bear. In 1944, prior to the discovery of Smokey Bear, the Forest Service and the National Advertising Council authorized a fire prevention poster by artist Albert Staehle, depicting a Smokey Bear. The popularity of the poster and the later inclusion of the real Smokey prompted Congress to pass a bill in 1952 to govern the commercialization of Smokey's name and image.

The Smokey Bear Museum and grave are at 118 West Smokey Bear Blvd. in Capitan. Admission is free. For more information, visit www .zianet.com/village/museum/museum.html or call (575) 354-2748.

More Bear Facts
Carlsbad

Maggie Oso is an artist. Although she's been practicing her skills for only a couple of years, her work commands some good prices. But what sets her apart from other artists is that Maggie is a bear.

She has been an artist-in-residence at the Living Desert Zoo and Gardens State Park for nearly three years, and her work is a big seller in the facility's gift shop. Maggie's journey to Carlsbad began in Georgia, where wildlife officials rescued her during a raid. She was in poor condition but recovered under the care of a wildlife reha- bilitation expert in Missouri. The rehabilitator and Living Desert Zoo hooked up over the Internet and Maggie arrived at her new home in August 2005.

Once accustomed to her surroundings, Maggie was introduced to the art world by Holly Payne, curator and caretaker at the zoo. Payne set out an array of nontoxic children's tempura paints next to several sheets of drawing paper. Maggie responded by slapping her paws into the paint. Then she walked across the papers that had

★ ★

"Maggie"nets
$2.00 each or 2/$3.00

Maggie Oso, the painting bear, creates
art with her paws near Carlsbad.

been strewn across the floor of her enclosure and *voila!* An artist was
born.

Using her paw-to-paper technique, Maggie creates bookmarks,
hair ties, small paintings, and large watercolors. The prices range
from less than $5 for smaller items to more than $100 for a major
work. Some of her paintings have been sold to collectors from all
across the country. All the proceeds benefit the Friends of the Living
Desert Zoo and Gardens.

Understandably, everything she produces is abstract. And,
although her works have won several blue ribbons at local art shows,

it should be pointed out that since she's the only bear artist, she's also the only one in her category. The lack of competition assures Maggie a blue ribbon every time.

The zoo is located on Country Road 435 off US 285, on the northwest edge north of Carlsbad. For more information, log on to www.emnrd.state.nm.us/PRD/LivingDesert.htm or call (575) 887-5516.

A Long Way Down—And Up
Carlsbad Caverns

Since Albuquerque is the largest city in New Mexico with more than 800,000 residents, it's logical to assume that Albuquerque would also have the tallest building in the state. It does. The twenty-two-story Albuquerque Plaza rises 351 feet, giving it the tallest designation by a wide margin.

And since that's the tallest building in the state, it's also logical to assume that it also has the longest elevator shaft in the state. It doesn't. The elevator that carries tourists from ground level to the primary viewing areas deep inside the Carlsbad Caverns National Park is more than twice as long as any other in all of New Mexico.

It's 750 feet one way, about the same height as a seventy-five-story building. Construction crews worked nearly eight months and used twelve tons of dynamite to blast the shaft in 1931. And the elevator they installed back then is still in use today. It travels at the rate of 9 miles per hour, so it takes a minute to go from top to bottom or vice versa.

Those with claustrophobia may use the Natural Entrance Route, which is longer in both time required and distance traveled. It's a self-guided tour for visitors with plenty of time and it's not recommended for the pot-of-bellied or weak-of-kneed because it's all downhill one way and all uphill the other way. The 1-mile hike traces the traditional explorers' route, and follows steep and narrow trails through a tall trunk passage known as the Main Corridor. Fortunately, it's well lit.

Either way, when the guests reach the bottom, they'll find what are probably the world's most subterranean snack bar and gift shop dispensing munchies and souvenirs more than one-sixth of a mile below the surface. Once the tummy and goodie bags are filled, there's still the Kings Palace Tour to explore. The ranger-guided walking excursions descend to the deepest part of the cavern, 830 feet down.

Taking the guided tour is optional and many choose to go it alone. It's another 1-mile walk that scrambles along paved pathways that go up and down as much as 80 feet before it's over. Regardless of which way they travel, those who go through Kings Palace will be surrounded by cave decorations naturally formed over millions of years in a most comfortable atmosphere because cavern temperatures are usually about 56 degrees Fahrenheit.

Once you reach the bottom level and start exploring the caverns, you'll want to whip out your camera and take photos of the stalactites and stalagmites, once you figure out which is which. (One easy way to remember is that stalactites—the formations that hang down from above—are spelled with a "c," which stands for "ceiling," and stalagmites—those that rise from below—are spelled with a "g," which stands for "ground.")

Because most of the spectacular formations are well lit by strategically placed floodlights, there's no need to use flash. But curiously, flash is also okay. This is rare in places like the caverns because of a fear that the bursts of light will damage the columns and pillars formed over the eons. But, according to the rangers here, those things have been there for so long that the flashes aren't going to hurt them.

You'll also notice that every now and then, you're going to get hit by a drop of water. This is not a cause for panic. The caverns don't create their own rain so you're not going to get caught in the middle of an underground downpour while the umbrella is up in the car. The drops are few and far between, and they're harmless. But they're also

★ ★

the reason behind the various shapes and forms because they were formed over the millennia by mineral deposits left by the individual drops of water.

This could possibly create the concern among worrywarts who fear they might be turned into a stalagmite (remember, they're the ones that spring up from the floor). Not to worry. It took more than 500,000 years of dripping to create the formations already here. It's doubtful that you or any other human being could stand perfectly still for that long.

And here's something else to put your mind at ease—you're not going to see everything. There are 113 caves in the park and more than 300 in the area so don't even think about it.

The Carlsbad Caverns are about 25 miles southwest of Carlsbad along U.S. Highway 62/180. For hours and information, contact the park at (505) 785-2232 or www.nps.gov/cave.

A Very Large Four-Legged Non-Spider
Carrizozo

Ask anyone in town where the McDonald Park is located and many of them won't know. But ask them where the Spider Park is, and nearly everyone has the correct answer.

It's a small patch of ground on the east side of the town's main drag through the heart of the community. And right in the heart of the park sits the spider. Actually, it's not a real spider, and it was never intended to even be mistaken for a spider. It's a concrete and lava rock sculpture that may have originally been designed as a fountain. Now they call it a monument. It has four arches that connect to a large rock cupola in the center. That, coupled with the dark brown coloration of the lava rock, gives it a tarantula-like appearance because the arches look like legs and the cupola looks like a spider body. A very big spider body.

In reality, however, the park is named after William C. McDonald, New Mexico's first governor after statehood. He served from 1912 to

1917. Although only a few can recall what made McDonald famous, his park must be held in some degree of reverence because there's a sign warning would-be spider riders that there's a $100 fine for climbing on the stone creature. Or maybe it's to caution people suffering from arachnophobia to keep their distance.

Big time arachnid hunters will find this giant on U.S. Highway 54 as it goes through Carrizozo, about 52 miles north of Alamogordo.

Those truly interested in the park's actual namesake will find his gravesite in White Oaks, a near-ghost town 12 miles northeast of Carrizozo on Highway 349.

. . . And the Burro You Rode In On

Carrizozo

When November comes to Carrizozo, it means the painted burros won't be far behind. They have been coming here every fall since 2006, and when they arrive, the streets become alive, lined with the colorful beasts of burden. They're green, red, orange, silver, gold, or black. And they're decorated with ancient signs, images of famous people, photographs, wings, or saddles. And a lot of other things.

The burros are life size but they're not real burros. Real burros would never stand still long enough to allow someone to paint a petroglyph on their bellies. In order to make an artistic statement, therefore, the burros that march in the annual Burro Serenade are aluminum.

Some past entries included *Incognito,* a Salvador Dali–like rendering by Michele Kay Caskey; *Donna Key-O-Key,* which resembled Pancho Sanza's ride; *Joan Glenn of the Alternate Species Space Administration,* a spoof of NASA by Timothy O'Lear and Allan Leslie; *Snapshot* by Vickie Caucutt, a donkey covered with photographs; and *Whimsey,* an orange donkey with a flower basket saddle by Joan Malkerson and Louise Groethe.

It all began in 2006 when Joan and Warren Malkerson, owners of Gallery 408, purchased twenty-two aluminum burros and then found

★ ★

(Poster courtesy of Joan Malkerson)

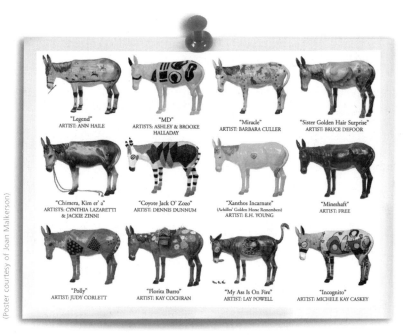

"Legend"
ARTIST: ANN HAILE

"MD"
ARTISTS: ASHLEY & BROOKE HALLADAY

"Miracle"
ARTIST: BARBARA CULLER

"Sister Golden Hair Surprise"
ARTIST: BRUCE DEFOOR

"Chimera, Kim er' a"
ARTISTS: CYNTHIA LAZARETTI & JACKIE ZINNI

"Coyote Jack O' Zozo"
ARTIST: DENNIS DUNNUM

"Xanthos Incarnate"
(Achilles' Golden Horse Remembers)
ARTIST: E.H. YOUNG

"Mineshaft"
ARTIST: FREE

"Polly"
ARTIST: JUDY CORLETT

"Florita Burro"
ARTIST: KAY COCHRAN

"My Ass Is On Fire"
ARTIST: LAY POWELL

"Incognito"
ARTIST: MICHELE KAY CASKEY

Life-size burros undergo major makeovers during a fiesta in Carrizozo.

twenty-two New Mexico artists to take them home and turn them into *objets d'art*. The number of burros and artists has increased every year. When completed, their works are returned to Carrizozo where they're put on display before being auctioned off. Many are purchased by local businesses and become permanent fixtures in stores and shops.

In the past bidders have parted with as much as $3,500 to take one of the colorful pets home. The money raised is donated to local charities. Old prospectors, burro collectors, and patrons of donkey art can visit the Malkersons at Gallery 408 on Twelfth Street. To get more information, log onto www.gallery408.com or call (575) 648-2598.

★ ★

Big Al and the Ghost

Cloudcroft

Those who seek the out-of-the-ordinary should consider a visit to this community nestled high in the Sacramento Mountains on US 82. There's a curiosity doubleheader waiting for them in the Lodge Resort and Spa.

First, there's the bar (the piece of furniture, not the building). It's about 30 feet long and made of hardwood. And it once belonged to Al Capone. The gangster had it built for his home in Cicero, a suburb of Chicago. It got to Cloudcroft because of a former owner of the Lodge. He collected mobster memorabilia and bought it at an auction, then trucked it out west in one piece. Now it serves those who belly up to it in Rebecca's, the resort lounge.

The bar is named Rebecca's in honor of the ghost who allegedly hangs around the place. According to the legend, the original Rebecca was a beautiful young chambermaid with deep blue eyes and flaming red hair. She disappeared from her quarters in the lodge one night many years ago, after her lumberjack boyfriend caught her in the arms of another man. No trace of her was ever found.

But that doesn't mean she's gone forever. According to the legend of the lodge, she still wanders the halls of the historic resort. She slides ashtrays across tables while the customers watch, opens and closes doors, moves furniture, and ignites logs in the fireplace. Barmaid Jane Tessler says she has had at least one encounter with Rebecca. She claims she walked into a storage area and saw a broom standing in the middle of the room, completely unsupported.

Tessler and the others who say they've seen the same thing weren't scared, however. They insist Rebecca is a friendly ghost and that none of her activities are either threatening or frightening. Perhaps, they say, she's just looking for another lover, or maybe she's checking out the portrait of herself that hangs in the lounge and appears on a brief history of the establishment given to all guests.

Believers, nonbelievers, and Casper fans can get more information by logging on to www.TheLodgeResort.com or by calling (800) 395-6343, or just pop in. The resort is located at 1 Corona Place. Turn south on Curfew Place as you enter Cloudcroft from the west and go about ½ mile.

A Rock Museum
Clovis

On the surface rock 'n' roll and Clovis would seem to be an incompatible pair. Clovis is in the heart of New Mexican ranching and oil country, not a typical venue for that kind of music. Despite that, the Norman and Vi Petty Rock 'n' Roll Museum was founded to highlight the city's surprisingly rich music history.

The museum, located in the basement of the Clovis Welcome Center and Chamber of Commerce at 105 East Grand, serves as a complement to the nearby Norman Petty 7th Street Studio, where such artists as Buddy Holly and the Crickets, Roy Orbison, Buddy Knox, Chita Rivera, Jimmy Gilmer and the Fireballs, and several others created the "Clovis sound" while recording there during the Fabulous Fifties. The studio no longer functions as a recording facility but it has been kept in its original condition with the big microphones dangling overhead, the original control board with large knobs, the wall clocks, and even a vintage Coca-Cola machine.

The studio, located at 1313 West Seventh Street, is open for tours but they must be booked in advance by calling the chamber of commerce. And those who really want to get the feel of it all might wander down the street to the Foxy Drive-In at 720 West Seventh Street. Holly and the Crickets used to devour large quantities of hamburgers there.

In 2007, the studio was presented with a New Mexico Scenic Historic Marker. It was the first roadside marker ever dedicated to rock 'n' roll music.

The museum-in-the-basement under the Welcome Center is designed to educate visitors about the process of re-creating a

working recording studio. It displays such artifacts as the original mixing board used to record Holly, photographs, an extensive radio collection, musical instruments, a theater area, and an old jukebox that plays songs from the early rock era. And, naturally, a gift shop.

If you're coming through town on U.S. Highway 60/84, go north on Main Street for 2 blocks to reach the welcome center. To see the studio and Foxy Drive-In, coming in on US 60/84 go north on Highway 270/Hull Street for 4 blocks to Seventh. For more information, log on to www.clovisnm.org or call the Clovis Chamber of Commerce at (575) 763-3435.

Fenced-In Choo-Choos
Clovis

A trip to the Clovis Depot Model Train Museum can be slightly confusing for the first-time visitor. It's easy enough to find because it's located in the former Atchison, Topeka and Santa Fe Railway depot, but there's a construction fence around it. So the newcomer might mistakenly assume that the place is closed and perhaps scheduled for demolition.

But the persistent will find the entrance on the north side of the building, away from the railroad tracks, and once inside they'll get the explanation about the fence. It was part of the sale transaction. When Phil and Vernah Williams bought the depot, they had to agree to fence it in to keep tourists and other visitors from wandering onto the tracks. Although there's no longer any passenger service, as many as one hundred freight trains still pass by every day.

The museum presents the history of toy trains in the United States, Great Britain, Australia, and the general Clovis area through a series of model trains chugging through nine miniature layouts. Some of the model buildings are converted birdhouses; others are pieces the owners have collected over the years.

The old depot has been restored to its 1950s appearance, and in 1996 was added to the National Register of Historic Places. And, because it remains in its original location, guests can get close-up views of the trains as they rumble past. Visitors can relive those golden days of belching locomotives during self-guided tours of the two-story facility. It's at 221 West First Street (also US 60/84), right behind the chain-link fence.

Because the hours of operation vary, it's best to get more information by logging on to www.clovisdepot.com or calling (888) 762-0064.

And don't worry about missing a train. One passes by almost every 15 minutes.

A Monument to Shame
Fort Sumner

Tepees are a common sight along New Mexico's roadways, but most of them have been placed there as advertising gimmicks for gift shops, trailer parks, and roadside attractions. They're made of sturdy cloth or concrete and most are not meant to last.

But the most magnificent of all is made of steel and has a truer and deeper purpose. It stands more than 20 feet tall and is the focal point of the $3.5 million visitor center at Bosque Redondo Memorial in Fort Sumner

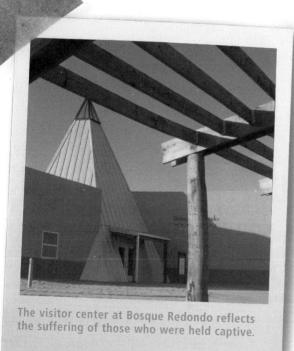

The visitor center at Bosque Redondo reflects the suffering of those who were held captive.

★ ★

A Desert Resting Place for Seafarers

Fort Stanton was established in 1855 as a frontier outpost and it served in that capacity until 1896. Around the turn of the 20th century, it was converted into a hospital for merchant marines suffering from tuberculosis. For many of the afflicted mariners, the fort became their final port. Their remains lie just across the road from the fort, in the only inland merchant marine cemetery in the United States.

State Park. The memorial commemorates one of this country's darkest hours, when more than 9,000 Navajos and Mescalero Apaches were forced off their tribal lands, forcibly marched 450 miles in the winter, and confined to the Bosque Redondo Reservation, a sprawling piece of ground surrounding Fort Sumner, an outpost built specifically to keep the natives on the reservation.

The situation lasted from 1862 until 1868, when the Indians were released and allowed to go home. Nearly one-third of them died during the ordeal. The Navajos still refer to the brutal treatment as "the Long Walk."

The building, designed by Navajo architect David Sloan, incorporates both the Apache tepee and the Navajo hogan into its design as a tribute to both tribes. The memorial grounds include the site where the Treaty of 1868, which released the Navajos from captivity, was signed. In the same area a small pile of rocks brought from the Navajo Reservation in 1971 honors those who were exiled here.

And during their confinement, the prisoners were forced to plant 12,000 cottonwood trees in the hope that they would eventually mature and provide firewood. Some of them are still standing, more than 140 years later.

Work on the monument started in 1991 as a memorial to truthfully acknowledge what happened here. Opened in 2005, it sits in the peacefully calm area about 6 miles southeast of the town of Fort Sumner. Take US 60 east to Billy the Kid Road, and then drive south for another 3 miles. For more information, log on to www.nmmonuments .org or call (505) 355-2573.

You Want Fries with That 3-Foot Bullet?

Fort Sumner

The Red Bandanna Cafe has a novel way of attracting customer attention—overkill.

A huge six-shooter invites diners into a restaurant in Fort Sumner.

The eatery has a big six-shooter stationed near its front door. It's huge. It's even bigger than that. It's enormous. The thing is about 10 feet long and stands about 5 feet tall, and the ammunition cylinder looks like it could hold a half dozen 3-foot cartridges.

But even though the legend of Billy the Kid is magnified over and over in this area, it's not a real gun. It's a barbecue grill. It hasn't been used to turn steers into dinner for several years, however, and now it just sits there, waiting to blast a 3-foot hole into anyone who doesn't stop for lunch.

The cafe is on the south side of US 60 at 1535 East Sumner Avenue, the town's main street. For information on how to get blasted, call (575) 355-9464.

Was It Cannibalism or Territorialism?

Hobbs

Most towns and cities have squirrels that give a sense of cuteness to parks, accept peanuts from strangers and cause near-accidents when they scurry across roads directly in front of traffic. But only a very few have tried something called "black squirrel boosterism."

Back in 1973, Hobbs attempted to become one of the few cities in the United States that could boast of a thriving black squirrel population, joining Council Bluffs, Iowa, which has had black squirrels since the 1840s, and Marysville, Kansas, which calls itself "the home of the black squirrels." Marysville is so proud of its little furballs that city adopted the black squirrel as its official mascot, holds an annual Black Squirrel Celebration, and commissioned the composition of "The Black Squirrel Song" as its official anthem.

Hobbs tried to join that elite group by borrowing several black squirrels from Marysville, hoping that they would establish a breeding colony in city parks. When the squirrels arrived, they were released into the pseudo-wild and told to go do whatever it is squirrels do to increase their population. It didn't work. Shortly after they were released, all the black squirrels were killed by the red fox squirrels the city had earlier imported from Texas.

Understandably, Marysville wasn't about to lend Hobbs any more black squirrels so the project went the way of the Edsel, the Ralph Nader presidential campaigns, and other notable failures.

And That Ain't No Bull
Hobbs

For several weeks in early 2008, something that looked like a Brahma bull kept watch over the parking lot at Forrest Tire Company at 1703 North Turner, which runs north off US 62/180 between Grimes Street and Highway 18. It had a hump like a Brahma, was the same color as a Brahma, and had horns like a Brahma, but it was only about half the size of a Brahma. Also, it was made of steel, with wheels where the hooves should have been.

So obviously, it wasn't a real Brahma.

It was a barbecue grill.

The inmates at the Lea County Correctional Facility built it and the resemblance to the real thing is almost uncanny, except, of course, for the panel that opened to put the coals inside the belly, and an area designed to hold condiments, beer, and other barbecuing essentials. After guarding the parking lot for a while, the creature was raffled off to raise money for the Hobbs United Way.

Eddie Solomon, the man in charge of project at the correctional facility, said the inmates have created a multitude of similar barbecues in the past. One was built to look like an old railroad locomotive. Another was a Christmas scene mounted on a trailer and brought in $7,500, which was donated to the Hobbs school system. They have also built barbecues that were raffled to benefit Little League baseball and the Lea County Motorcycle Toy Run.

It's a Coca-Cola Thing

Hobbs

Those who enter Casey's, a restaurant owned and operated by Paula Manis, might find it hard to believe that she doesn't drink any more Coca-Cola than the average person because she is a Coke collector of the highest order.

Casey's is a veritable museum that houses the Coca-Cola memorabilia Mrs. Manis has been amassing since 1986. And it's more than Coke bottles. She has every Coca-Cola village ever produced, along with all the people. She has the Coke ads that appeared in *National Geographic* from the 1930s through the 1970s. She has Super Bowl Coke bottles, March Madness Coke bottles, and 215 Coke puzzles.

The windows of her restaurant feature the Coca-Cola polar bears and people in Coca-Cola Christmas tableaus. She has Coke-dispensing machines, including one that was left to her in the will of a woman who wanted Mrs. Manis to have it instead of her own children. She doesn't keep a precise count of her artifacts but estimates there are more than 5,000 Coke-related items in the four rooms of her eatery, plus another seven boxes of Coke stuff she can't put on display because there's no room. Among them are Coke playing cards, marbles, cigarette lighters, ashtrays, paper dolls, and bottles bearing the logos of professional athletic teams.

"People just keep bringing Coke stuff in," Mrs. Manis said, "and we take anything."

"Anything" includes Coke place mats, Coke napkins, and Coke writing instruments.

Caffeine lovers and others can find Casey's at 209 West Broadway. Coming into town on US 62/180, go north on Grimes Street, take a right on Broadway, and go 6 blocks to the restaurant on your right. And anyone who has an old Coca-Cola washing machine or log cabin they want to donate can call (575) 393-0308. Just try not to burp into the phone.

Why There's Only a Little Hope

Hope

The last census indicated that 107 people reside in Hope, a town west of Artesia. It's been at that level for a long time, and it doesn't look like the future is going to bring much more growth except for retirees and those who want to get away from the big city. During its peak days, however, around the turn of the twentieth century, it had a population of nearly 7,000 people who raised apples, alfalfa, dairy cattle, and walnuts. The town boasted a hotel, bank, and schools, and the people irrigated their fields with water from the Penasco River. Life was good.

And there was a lot of Hope.

But then, according to the story told by current residents, in the early 1900s the town fathers decided they could draw more water from the river if they deepened the channel. However, because the riverbed was so rocky, they couldn't merely dig into it by hand or any of the equipment available at the time so they had to use dynamite. Bad decision. The dynamite blasted a hole in the riverbed and all the water drained into an aquifer 600 feet below. This made the river unusable for irrigation so the crops dried up and many people left town.

And there was hardly any Hope left.

But then there was supposed to be new Hope.

The Santa Fe Railway announced it would extend a spur into the community to give farmers a better access to the markets. That hope for Hope vanished, however, because the money for the project was on the *Titanic* when it sank. Or so the story goes.

So now there's only a little Hope.

Those who drive a couple miles out of town in either direction find themselves beyond Hope. Those who have lost Hope will find it again on US 82 about 20 miles west of Artesia.

★ ★

A Name Spelled Out in Water

Jal

The actual origins of why Jal is called Jal are a little sketchy but most agree that it was named after the brand on a herd of cattle brought to the area by the Cowden family around 1885. What—or who—the brand stood for remains debatable. Some versions say it represented the initials of a Texas cattleman but they're not sure if it was John A. Lynch, John A. Lawrence or J. A. Lee. Another story claims the Jal stood for the first names of three Cowden brothers—James, Amos, and Lidden.

But one thing is certain: Jal is the only town in the nation—maybe even the whole world—that has a lake shaped in the form of its name. The initialized body of water is located in a ten-acre park on

Postcard image courtesy of Jal City Hall

Jal may be the only city in the world
with its name in a lake.

★ ★

the south side of the community. However, those who go there expecting to get a liquid spelling lesson will be disappointed because both the park and the lake surface are very flat and there are no elevated vantage points. So the only way to get the full impact is to fly over the lake in some sort of airborne vehicle.

It's a lot easier—and a whole lot cheaper—to go to the Jal City Hall at 309 Main, which can best be reached by going west on Utah Avenue off Highway 18. At the city hall you can pick up a free post-card that shows an aerial view of the brand-in-a-lake. But be sure to hold it right side up when looking at it. If held upside down, the lake sort of resembles a jock strap.

And here's something else interesting—according to the official publication distributed by the Chamber of Commerce, "the town rests 8 miles *north* of the Texas border and 7 miles *west* of the Texas border." Is that a misprint?

Nope. It's just the way Texas wraps around that corner of New Mexico.

A True Jal Gal

Jal

Jal doesn't have a historical museum yet but it already has a great donation—a set of golf clubs. What makes them worthy of inclusion in a museum is that they once belonged to Kathy Whitworth, a Hall of Fame golfer who calls Jal her hometown.

She grew up here and graduated from Jal High School in 1957. The locals often relate the story about how she became a golfer by accident. Tennis was her first love, but one day the courts were full so some friends talked her into playing golf instead. The rest is what movie scripts are made of: She took up the game seriously, playing with her grandmother's old clubs. Since the high school didn't have a girls' golf team, her parents joined the country club, and she took les-sons from a pro. Then her mother frequently drove her 500 miles to Austin, Texas, so she could train under Harvey Penick.

After winning two state amateur championships, Whitworth turned pro at age nineteen, and within three years she had earned her first victory and was ranked second on the money list. She won 10 tournaments in 1968 and eight each in 1963, 1965, 1966 and 1967. In 1981 she became the first female golfer to pass $1 million in career earnings, and when she retired in 1993, she had recorded eighty-eight tour victories, more than any other professional golfer, male or female.

Memorabilia tracing her accomplishments are currently on display in the Woolworth Community Library, located at the corner of Third Street and Utah Avenue (take Utah west off of Highway 18). They'll join her golf clubs when the museum—still in the planning stages—is built.

The library, incidentally, is absolutely amazing. It's a very large architectural masterpiece, set into a sloping area and carefully designed to utilize natural lighting. One section is devoted to the memory of the Woolworth family, major benefactors of the library. One wall of the Woolworth Room is lined with boards from the family's longtime residence.

The library—and Kathy Whitworth's golf clubs—are at the corner of Third and Utah Streets. For information call (505) 395-3268.

Silhouetted Cowboys
Jal

The landscape in these parts is relatively flat so the skyline is almost a straight line drawn across the horizon. The levelness is broken only by hundreds of oil rigs, large devices resembling monster-sized praying mantises that bob up and down, continuously kissing the earth and then the sky while sucking the precious liquid from the depths.

But then the cowboys appear.

A couple of miles north of town, the critters and cowboys in a metal sculpture entitled "The Trail Ahead" loom over the flatlands in the form of giant silhouettes. It's a Western scene done in ¼-inch steel, and features thirteen cows and four mounted cowboys. They're all huge. Even gigantic. A 6-foot man comes up to just below the horses' bellies. One of the cowboys rises more than 20 feet above the ground, and some of the cows are more than 15 feet long. When viewed from a distance,

they look like humungous black cutouts, but closer inspection reveals that they're a rusted brown.

Twenty-foot tall cowboys dominate the landscape near Jal.

Brian Norwood, the sculptor, has been around Jal for several years, making a living as an artist, but this was his first attempt at cutting figures out of steel. He relied on old photographs for the outlines and then used a plasma torch to cut them. And he did it well enough that several old-timers claim they recognize the men depicted, even though they are only steel shapes with no identifying features.

Those who can't live without a close-up of the Old West done in outline and profile can reach the sculpture by taking Third Street north from downtown Jal, turning west on Phillips Hill Road, and then going south on a dirt road for ¼ mile to the site.

★ ★

Norwood is also responsible for the Hobbs Army Air Field B-17 Project, a life-size metal silhouette of the famed World War II bomber, also cut from quarter-inch steel and placed in the Hobbs Industrial Air Park, site of the former Hobbs Army Air Field. From 1942 to 1946, the air field served as a transitional training base where pilots learned to fly four-engine bombers, including the B-17.

The sculpture stands 19 feet high and stretches more than 78 feet. For more information, contact Norwood at bgnorwood75@valornet .com or call him at (505) 441-7391.

Bomber on a Pole
Lea County

An unusual, but extremely eye-catching, tribute to American service-men breaks the monotony of the level ground between mile markers 23 and 24 on Highway 18 south of Hobbs.

It's a replica of a jet bomber, painted in bright colors and mounted on a steel pole about 10 feet off the ground. Underneath, an inscrip-tion cut into a steel plate reads: "Cherish your freedom. It did not come free. Always remember those Americans who sacrificed so much for it."

Technically, the bomber is a miniature but it's pretty big, measur-ing more than 20 feet long with a 30-plus-foot wingspan. There are no identifying marks anywhere on the work, and it sits in an isolated area so there's nobody around to answer any inquiries. It's just there. And noticeable. And pretty impressive.

A Kid Named Billy
Lincoln County (and almost everywhere else)

Briefly, according to historical documents, this is what happened.

Henry McCarty was born in New York, November 23, 1859 or 1860, to Catherine McCarty and a father whose name has been lost in history. Catherine McCarty and her two sons moved to

Should this be small caps, since it's a sign?

★ ★

Indianapolis, where she met William Antrim. They were married in Santa Fe and moved to Silver City, where Catherine died of tuberculosis. Young Henry's life of crime began shortly afterward when he was arrested but escaped. The incident set the pattern for the remainder of his life.

He killed a man named Windy Cahill in Fort Grant, Arizona, on August 17, 1877, and was charged with "a criminal and unjustifiable shooting." He escaped from jail and fled to New Mexico, where, over the years, he went under the names of William Bonney and Henry "Kid" Antrim, and some called him El Chivato. He fought in the Lincoln County War, allegedly shot and killed several more men, became a legend, and was slain by Sheriff Pat Garrett on July 14, 1881.

End of story?

No way.

Although only one actual photograph of Billy the Kid is known to exist, his image appears on book covers, wanted posters, and historical documents.

★ ★

Since then, Billy the Kid has entered the realm of immortality, sustained by a combination of myth, folklore, and legend that occasionally includes some actual fact. He has been the subject of movies, novels, and scientific studies. He is honored in museums, has roads and stores named after him, and maintains a position of historical prominence more than 120 years after his death.

Much of his story is well detailed, but here are a few Billy the Kid items of a nature so unusual that they deserve inclusion in any publication dealing with the curious:

- Billy has been the subject of more than sixty movies (the folks at the museum in Fort Sumner say it's more than 150 when you include foreign films). He has been portrayed by such screen luminaries as Johnny Mack Brown, Roy Rogers, Robert Taylor, Lash La Rue, Buster Crabbe, Rocky Lane, Bob Steele, Jack Buetel, Audie Murphy, Don "Red" Barry, Scott Brady, Nick Adams, Anthony Dexter, Paul Newman, Emilio Estevez, Michael J. Pollard, and Kris Kristofferson. And also by a few lesser-knowns: Dean White, Tyler MacDuff, Jack Taylor, Johnny Ginger, Chuck Courtenay, Peter Lee Lawrence, Gaston Sands, Geoffrey Deuel, and Jean-Pierre Léaud.

- His grave site, located on an isolated patch of ground adjacent to the Old Fort Sumner Museum, is surrounded by iron bars, a possible case of symbolic irony since iron bars could never hold him during his lifetime. But more probably, they're designed to keep tourists from tromping on his grave. There's no admission fee for the site, and Billy isn't the only one buried there. In fact, he's not the only one buried inside the iron bars. His pals Tom O'Follaird and Charlie Bowdre are lined up in adjacent graves. At least twenty other burial sites share the rest of the cemetery. One of them holds the remains of Lucien Maxwell, father of Pete Maxwell, owner of the house in which Billy met his fate.

- The grave site is southeast of Fort Sumner. On Billy the Kid Road.

- References to Billy pop up everywhere. The plaque adjacent to a bronze statue of famed cattleman John Chisum in Roswell points out that Chisum was a member of the committee that hired Pat Garrett to get rid of Billy. Dowlin's Historic Old Mill in Ruidoso was "reported to be a hangout of Billy the Kid." Billy the Kid Springs in Chaves County northwest of Kenna "was one of Billy the Kid's hideouts." The schedule of events for the annual Old Lincoln Days always includes "a re-enactment of the last escape of Billy the Kid."

- The *New Mexico Vacation Guide* has a section entitled "Billy the Kid's Stomping Grounds."

- During a 2007 Billy the Kid exhibition in the Albuquerque Museum of Art and History, guests were asked to vote on whether or not Billy should be pardoned. The vote was more than two to one in his favor.

- The brochure for the exhibition noted that Billy loved to dance and his favorite tune was "Turkey in the Straw."

- One of the displays in the Ramah historical museum is a photo of old-time residents. Among them is John Miller, who lived in the area for years and claimed he was Billy the Kid. Miller, a key figure in the book, *Whatever Happened to Billy the Kid?*, by Helen Airy, lived on a ranch in Miller Canyon. According to local historians, his neighbors knew who he was but didn't turn him in because they either liked him or were afraid of him.

- Billy as an artist's model: The outlaw's image is preserved in tile and a wooden cutout at the Ruidoso Downs Visitor Center; in a life-size wood carving at the entry and a steel silhouette atop a machine that smashes pennies into souvenirs at

Billy the Kid's grave site is surrounded by iron bars to make sure he finally stays put.

the Billy the Kid Museum in Fort Sumner; and in oil paintings on the walls, in weaving on a floor mat, and in neon on the sign at the Billy the Kid Casino in Ruidoso Downs.

- The Lincoln County Courthouse in Lincoln is now a museum. On April 28, 1881, while being held in the courthouse awaiting execution, Billy killed two deputies during an escape. The history of that episode includes the notation that he hung around the courthouse for a while, talking with the townspeople, and then stole a horse and rode out of town. Later, so the story goes, he came back into Lincoln to return the horse. A replica of the courthouse has been created inside the Billy the Kid Casino.

- An article in a *New Mexico Travelers Guide 2008* tourism magazine observes that visitors to the Lincoln State Monument "can walk in the footsteps of Billy the Kid (and) Pat Garrett. . . ."

- A brochure extolling the tourist attractions in and around Ruidoso notes that the Miner's Home and Tool Shed Museum in White Oaks is right next to the cemetery that is "the resting spot for . . . deputy Tom Bell (killed by Billy the Kid when he escaped from the Lincoln County Courthouse)."

- Brochures are big on promoting Billy. One observes that "open animosity between the two (competing) factions would eventually lead into the Lincoln County War and the rise of the infamous Billy the Kid." Another exclaims, "In 1878, the Lincoln County War catapulted into legend a young cowboy who went by the name of Billy the Kid." Still another proclaims that Billy was twenty-one years old when he died and "legend has it that he killed 21 men." And Fort Sumner's brochures tout it as "the International Billy the Kid Capital."

- Among the 60,000 relics on display in the Billy the Kid Museum are his rifle, chaps, spurs, and a variety of newspaper articles about men who claimed they were Billy the Kid, claimed they knew Billy the Kid personally, claimed they helped bury Billy the Kid, and claimed they helped Billy the Kid hide out because Garrett didn't actually kill him. Another area is filled with such historical items as a copy of the death sentence handed down after he killed a lawman, a Billy "wanted" poster framed in a horse harness, poems dedicated to his memory, and a book bearing the title, *Billy the Kid: The Good Side of a Bad Man.*

- People who don't get to see everything in the Billy the Kid Museum in one day can stay overnight in the Billy the Kid Country Inn, conveniently located directly across the street.

- The Billy the Kid Scenic Byway starts at the Billy the Kid Visitor Center in Ruidoso Downs, and then loops through Hondo,

Lincoln, Fort Stanton, and Capitan before ending in Ruidoso. Just follow the signs with Billy's image on them.

- The only known photograph of Billy the Kid was a tintype taken by a traveling photographer in 1880. Because pictures made from a tintype produced mirror images, the photo led to the mistaken belief that Billy was left-handed. So in 1939, when Metro-Goldwyn-Mayer decided to make the movie *Billy the Kid,* studio officials demanded that Billy's portrayer, Robert Taylor, learn to handle a gun with his left hand even though most of the story was pure fiction. But when old cowboy actor William S. Hart showed them a photo of Billy as a right-hander, the way it actually was, MGM's bosses opted to leave their version of Billy as a southpaw, probably because they had invested so much time and effort in left-handed quick-draw lessons for their star.

To Honor a Gridiron Great
Lovington

Brian Urlacher is big here, in more ways than one. He not only has a big reputation, but his countenance covers a billboard and the entire side of a downtown building. He is the local hero, the epitome of a hometown boy who made good. It's all because of his ability to play a game that has as its major component an air-filled ball made of pigskin.

Urlacher is a football player and a pretty darned good one. He became a star at Lovington High School, where he was named New Mexico's high school player of the year in 1995. Following gradua-tion, he starred at New Mexico University, where he was the Player of the Year in the Mountain West Conference and was picked on three All-America teams.

Chicago's National Football League team drafted Urlacher ninth in 2000. Since then, he has been a mainstay at middle linebacker, was

Not His Favorite Place

Lew Wallace served as a general in the Union army during the Civil War, practiced law in Indiana, and tried his hand at writing before he was appointed governor of the Territory of New Mexico in 1878. He accepted the post at the urging of President Rutherford B. Hayes, primarily because he thought it would lead to a higher government position.

Wallace's time in New Mexico was notable for several reasons. He inherited the Lincoln County War and, in an effort to settle it, he enlisted the aid of Billy the Kid, who wrote Wallace that he had witnessed the murder of one of the principals. Wallace promised the Kid a full pardon for his past misdeeds, and several men were indicted as a result of his testimony. But none was ever tried and the district attorney in charge of the situation informed Wallace that he had no intention of granting the pardon. Faced with a hangman's noose, Billy rode out of Lincoln and went on to greater things.

Wallace would later sign a death warrant for the Kid after his capture at Mesilla. Billy wrote Wallace to remind him of his promise, but the governor ignored his pleas and told a reporter, "I can't see how a fellow like him should expect any clemency from me." Billy made it a non-issue by escaping.

Also during his time as governor, Wallace returned to his writing and penned a novel entitled *Ben-Hur: A Tale of the Christ.* It became a best seller and has twice been made into a movie. It was also his ticket out of New Mexico because once he became a well-known author, President James A. Garfield appointed him ambassador to Turkey.

Despite that, Wallace never liked the state. He once commented: "Every calculation based on experience elsewhere fails in New Mexico." His wife, Susan, was fond of the state at first but later recommended in a letter to one of her sons that the United States make Mexico take New Mexico back.

★ ★

Lovington's football hero Brian Urlacher is well-remembered in his hometown.

named Defensive Rookie of the Year and Defensive Player of the Year, and has been invited to the Pro Bowl six times. During his first seven years with the Bears, he racked up 838 tackles and assists and 37.5 sacks.

Lovington honors this favorite son with the billboard bearing his photo and credentials on Highway 18 south of town, and a small shrine in the Lovington Chamber of Commerce. And, of course, that 20-foot tall face that covers the side of that building.

Although he no longer lives here, Urlacher comes back frequently to check on his automobile dealership and to play in a charity basketball game.

Incidentally, sports analysts who insist on referring to outstanding football players as "animals" have a pretty good example in Urlacher. During his career he has starred for the Lovington High School Wildcats, the University of New Mexico Lobos, and now the Chicago Bears.

Hi Yo Iguana!
Lovington

Pssst. Hey, you. You, carrying the salamander under your arm. Yeah, you. Wanna know how to make that lizard run faster?

Tickle him with a feather.

Don't snicker. That bit of knowledge has pushed such reptiles as Fred Zard, Miss Hissy Fit, and Lizard Snaily to victory in the annual Great Lizard Race.

The event is held every year as part of the city's Fourth of July celebration and has drawn as many as thirty-six lizards who run as fast as they can (or as fast as they darn well want to) along tracks laid out in a big sandbox while their owners stroke them with feathers. It's the only form of human intervention allowed, although race officials point out that they have never checked the racers for steroids.

Fred Zard, an iguana, became part of lizard-racing lore a few years ago when his owner drove 908 miles one way from Lakeside, California, to compete. Fred won first place in his category but, as race officials are quick to mention, he was the only iguana entered so obtaining the first-place ribbon was a cinch. Partially because of that incident, there's no on-track betting during lizard races.

Winners get cash and merchandise prizes. Losers get to stick out their tongues and hiss about waiting until next year. For details on how to get your creepy crawler onto the track, call the Lovington Chamber of Commerce at (505) 396-5311, or visit http://lovington coc.org/.

A Sportswriters Dream
Pep

Both Pep and Dunken are very small communities in southeastern New Mexico. They're so small they don't have schools. This is a misfortune for sportswriters. If the towns did have schools, they'd also have athletic teams. And if they had athletic teams, the teams would have nicknames. So if squads from these two towns were to play each other, it could possibly result in a contest between the Pep Peronis and the Dunken Donuts.

Just think of the fun a reporter would have trying to write about that game without breaking up.

Pep is about 25 miles south of Portales on Highway 206, and Dunken is about halfway in between Alamogordo and Artesia, about 10 miles south of US 82 on Highway 24.

There's Something in the Wind
Portales

Bill Dalley isn't sure why it happened, but he does remember the day he started collecting windmills. It was in the 1970s and he went to a friend's abandoned farmstead, looking for old lumber he could use for woodworking. During the search, he found an old windmill, asked about it, and was told he could have it. So he dragged it home. "It just tickled my wife to death," he says with a chuckle, "but after a while, she got used to me bringing them home."

Now, more than 25 years after this first acquisition, Dalley's rural home is surrounded by windmills, and many of them still creak, spin and groan. They're not all complete windmills. Some are sitting on their original stands; others are merely fans and blades. They range in size from standard to extra large, with some of the fans measuring up to 8 feet across. Regardless of what shape they're in, he has 86 of them, collected from all across New Mexico and west Texas and brought to his home in the back of a pickup truck.

It's still a hobby, Dalley says, and not a windmill museum. But curious passersby and serious windmill fans are all welcome to stop at his place and refresh their memories about the good old days when these wind-powered machines not only pumped water but also acted as grain-grinding mills.

In fact, windmills once meant survival to the farmers and ranchers who fought to make the high arid desert livable. They sucked water from deep wells and provided sustenance not only to humans, but also to the water-guzzling steam engines so vital to success back in the old days.

His collection is on display day and night on his twenty-acre spread, located east of Portales two miles south of U.S. Highway 70 on Kilgore Road. There's no charge for stopping and looking and most days, Dalley will be on the grounds to conduct a personal tour, which is valuable because he knows each windmill personally and can usually relate at least a part of its background.

Something for You Snarly Fans
Portales

One of the items in Bill Dalley's collection looks like a windmill having a bad hair day. The fan is almost obscured by a tangled mass of rusted wire, and there's a similar grouping lower down on the wooden obelisk that supports the unit.

Dalley says they're raven nests.

Close inspection reveals that the masses are composed of short pieces of wire that have been skillfully intertwined to form what appears to be a nest. Even closer inspection reveals remnants of feathers lining the centers of the wiry amalgamations. This gives credibility to Dalley's belief that they were created by either ravens or crows, who wove the bits of wire into a place they could call home, definitely a place safe enough to raise the kids.

Grooming the Legumes
Portales

Peanuts are a major crop in this area's agriculture industry, and local plants process millions of pounds every year. At Sunland Inc., for example, workers turn about 55 million pounds of peanuts into eighteen different kinds of peanut butter, including banana peanut butter, raspberry peanut butter, caramel peanut butter, and cinnamon peanut butter.

A large panel inside Sunland's lobby explains the growing process thusly:

The peanut plants flower in April, and when the flowers die, each spot left by a blossom sends out a shoot called a "peg," and each peg implants itself into the ground and produces a peanut. Then in October, the plants are uprooted and turned to expose the mature peanuts, which are sun dried and harvested.

But the interesting thing about peanuts is that they're not nuts. They're legumes, like beans and peas. This poses the question: If they're legumes, why are they called nuts? There's no definitive answer but it probably has something to do with semantics. After all, the general public might be a little reluctant to order a "pealegume butter and jelly sandwich."

And think of the ballpark vendors shouting, "Pealegumes! I gotchyer hot, roasted pealegumes heeyah!"

Botanists, vegetarians, and legume lovers who need more information can view the process at Sunland Inc., 42593 US 70. Call (575) 356-6638, www.sundlandinc.com for tour times and appointments.

Note: As an apparent tribute to the peanut's alternative name, the goober, there's a bar in Portales named Goober McCool's. It's at 1604 South Avenue D, but they don't make goober martinis.

An Airborne Deliverer
Queen

Long before computers and cable television provided instant access to the major events of the day, newspapers were the prime source of information. They were published in almost every city, town, and hamlet and, in most cases, were delivered by young males known as "paperboys."

★ ★

Frank Kindel was one of them. But he wasn't young. And he was delivering papers long after most paperboys had matured and moved on to better-salaried jobs. Also, he didn't walk his paper route—he delivered the news by air.

His customers consisted mainly of ranchers located in the rugged Guadalupe Mountains northwest of Carlsbad. Kindel delivered the papers by dropping them from his Piper Cruiser as he flew over the ranches. According to some rather sketchy information on his life, he was still on the job well into his fifties, and his final flight came in 1964 when he crashed his plane in the mountains after flying a minister to a sunrise service. He was seventy-one.

There's a monument in the Guadalupes honoring his life and achievements. On the base of a 10-foot obelisk made of stone and concrete with a small metal propeller attached to the front, a plaque says it's a memorial to Frank Kindel, "The Flying Paper Boy of the Guadalupes." The plaque also declares that he lived from October 30, 1892, until May 31, 1964, and that he "lived a life of service dedicated to his family, his community and his fellow man."

On the last day of his life, the plaque relates, "he flew across the great divide into eternity when his plane crashed near this spot in the Lincoln National Forest."

The monument is located almost 35 miles northwest of Carlsbad. To get there, take US 285 north of Carlsbad for 15 miles to Highway 137 and then drive west into the Lincoln National Forest for 20 miles. It's a fairly long round-trip so be sure to fill the gas tank and lay in a supply of liquid and snacks before venturing forth because, although Queen appears on some maps, there's not much there.

The Curiosity Capitol

Roswell

All across New Mexico, any inquiry into the weird, the unusual, the curious, the strange, and the out-of-the-ordinary is commonly met with the same answer: "Roswell."

★ ★

Little green men act as pitchmen in the
windows of Roswell souvenir shops.

Or, sometimes, the question is answered with a question: "Have
you been to Roswell?"

The inference is well deserved. Roswell is different, and it's
because of the well-publicized incident of July 8, 1947. Briefly, this is
what happened:

A rancher came across the wreckage of what appeared to be an
alien spacecraft. He reported it to authorities and the U.S. Air Force

issued a press release declaring that debris from a crashed "flying disc" had been recovered near the ranching community of Corona.

An international media storm followed and the Air Force quickly retracted the original statement and said the wreckage was actually an experimental weather balloon. Officials stuck to that story for more than thirty years and then disclosed that it was part of a top-secret effort to monitor Soviet-era nuclear testing. But many still believe that a UFO did crash and that the federal government is covering it up. Some even maintain that the military recovered an alien body near the crash site, but the rumor is met with repeated government denials.

It since has evolved into the "Roswell Incident" and the city has taken up the cause with substantial enthusiasm. Reminders and spin-offs of the episode are everywhere. Here are a few notables:

- Since opening in 1992, the International UFO Museum and Research Center has greeted more than 2.5 million visitors who pump an estimated $35 million in direct and indirect spending each year into the local economy. The museum is currently housed in an old movie theater but is planning to move into a newer, larger building a few blocks away.

The UFO Museum takes it all seriously and draws visitors by the millions, almost all of them earthlings.

- One of the exhibits in the museum is a life-size fiberglass horse covered with news clippings about the incident and the ongoing debate. Across the room is the set of an alien autopsy scene from the 1994 television movie *Roswell*. It depicts an operating room where doctors prepare to examine an emaciated alien corpse.

- The mailbox in front of the Roswell Visitor Center has been painted to resemble either a space ship or R2-D2, the 'droid from the *Star Wars* movies.

- The front of a local McDonald's is shaped like a flying saucer. Other alien-themed eateries include the Not of This World coffeehouse and the Cover Up Cafe. And Arby's has a sign out front that says Welcome Aliens.

- Aliens as art: A large oil painting depicting what may or may not have happened in 1947 covers most of one wall in the museum; a one-dimensional steel sculpture outside shows

Clever use of metal slats has created an alien face on a chain-link fence.

★ ★

rancher Mack Brazel, who discovered the wreckage, astride a horse and surrounded by debris that includes an alien. A neon light shaped like an alien directs visitors to the museum at night. The parking lot at a mini mall has an alien cast in concrete directing cars. A chain-link fence along Main Street has green and black slats cleverly inserted into the links to create an alien head.

- Aliens as advertising gimmicks: At least two Coca Cola machines in the downtown area feature a green alien drinking green Coke from a green bottle. Starchild, a gift and souvenir shop, displays white aliens and a spaceship above the entryway. Roswell Landing, another souvenir dispensary, has an alien-manned spaceship painted across the storefront.

- The Alien Zone features an exhibit entitled "Area 51," where 3-foot-high aliens strike such human poses as reading a newspaper and sitting in a jail cell, while others do more alien-oriented things like stumbling around the wreck of a spaceship and undergoing surgery by humans.

- Roswell officials and residents are studying a proposal by entrepreneurs who want to build a $76 million resort and conference center for UFO enthusiasts. It would be called "Earth Station Roswell" and would feature a concert center, restaurants, lounge, lecture hall, and theater. The centerpiece would be "Mothership," a seven-story, 200-room hotel that would be, according to the designers, "the world's largest replica of a flying saucer."

- A vacant lot displays a sign that warns UFO PARKING ONLY and gift shops sell T-shirts with such messages as "Aliens Rule" and "Aliens (the other gray meat). Gotta love 'em. They taste just like chicken."

★ ★

The message is clear, but a lot of human vehicles park there anyway.

- The Wal-Mart logo on the building front incorporates an alien into its design, and many of the store's windows show aliens shopping for food, reading newspapers, and trying out fishing poles.

- The Roswell UFO Festival annually draws thousands of believers and skeptics who discuss deep space and deep thinking with UFO-logists and sci-fi movie actors.

- The globes on streetlights along Main Street have been painted with slanty eyes so they resemble out-of-spacers, and one of the participants in the city's hot air balloon festival looks like a giant air-filled green head from another galaxy.

Need more convincing that Roswell has earned its reputation? Log on to www.roswellnm.org or call (877) 849-7679. But don't expect a Klingon to answer. Even in Roswell, that's just a bit too much.

How Far Down Is Down?
Roswell

Bottomless Lakes was New Mexico's first state park, but the bodies of water so designated are neither bottomless nor lakes. None is more than 90 feet deep, and they're sinkholes.

They were formed when underground water dissolved the salt and gypsum deposits to form subterranean caverns, then the caverns collapsed when they were unable to support their own weight, and the resulting sinkholes were soon filled with water.

The "bottomless" label was attached more than a century ago by cowboys driving cattle along a nearby trail. The cowpunchers tied rocks to their lariats and dropped them into the lakes. When one length of rope played out, they attached another but they never hit bottom, hence the name. But the reason they didn't reach bottom was that their crude depth gauges were being swept away by underwater currents. Being cowboys and not scientists, the cattle herders had no way of knowing that. However, adding some credibility to the name was an unsubstantiated story that two young people drowned in one of the lakes and their bodies were later found in the Carlsbad Caverns, nearly 100 miles away.

The park is located 12 miles east of Roswell on US 380, then 7 miles north on Highway 409.

A Rare Mini Cave
Roswell

The cave responsible for giving the Cactus Cave Gift Shop its name isn't really a cave. It's an aboveground shell composed of rocks and

★ ★

dirt. But it looks like a dinky little cave and amateur spelunkers can, if they so choose, crawl into it. They can even explore it, if they don't mind stooping over and crawling around on their hands and knees.

The faux cave was built back in the 1980s by the original owner of the shop, who used dirt and rocks scraped from the surround- ing landscape. It looks more like a shrine than a cave, and there's a religious icon that even stands inside. But the current owners say nobody comes there to pray. In fact, a tepee on the other side of the parking lot attracts more attention than the cave.

Both are visible at the shop, located on the north side of US 380 about 2 miles west of Roswell.

A Parade of Dinosaurs
Roswell

Finding the Eastern New Mexico State Fairgrounds is no problem. Just look for the fence composed of farm machinery from bygone days.

The old equipment ranges from a rusted threshing machine to a hay rake to a seeder. About a dozen of them stand in silent testi- mony to the way things used to be, forming a fence along the west- ern edge of the fairgrounds. Like many other things that once served useful purposes, they are now extinct and have become museum pieces.

The elderly machinery and the fairgrounds are at 2500 SE Main/US 285 on the southern edge of Roswell.

Hard to Spell, Harder to Pronounce
Ruidoso

Here's the thing a lot of people don't realize about Ruidoso—the cor- rect pronunciation, according to a sign hanging in the Visitor Center, is "ROO-ee-DOH-so."

However, those who say it that way apparently are in the minor- ity. As a woman in a local business place explained, "I've lived here for thirty years and it's always been 'Rio-DOH-so' to me and I'm not going to change now."

An informal and very unscientific poll conducted along the city's main street indicates that "rio-DOH-so" is the mispronunciation of preference. However, the survey also revealed "Roo-doh-so," "Roo-dee-doh-so," "Ree-doh-so," and "Roo-dee-oh-so" renditions.

Ruidoso comes from "rio ruidoso," Spanish for "noisy water."

Here are a couple more things most people don't know about Ruidoso—Neil Patrick Harris grew up here and Ross Anderson lives and works here.

Harris, a noted television and movie performer, got his acting start when he appeared as Toto in an elementary school production of *The Wizard of Oz.* He later achieved a great deal of success as television's *Doogie Howser, M.D.,* then starred in such movies as *Harold and Kumar Go to White Castle, Clara's Heart, Purple People Eaters,* and *Starship Troopers.* Harris has also appeared in Broadway productions, including *Sweeney Todd* and *RENT.* Since the 2004-05 seasons, he has had a leading role in the television series *How I Met Your Mother.*

Anderson, a Native American, is a speed skier, the best in American history. In 2001, he became the first minority skier to win a major award in Alpine sport, finishing second in the Champion de Monde in Les Arcs, France. And then, in 2006, he was clocked at 154.06 miles per hour on a downhill run, making his the ninth fastest time ever recorded in the sport anywhere in the world.

When not burning up the slopes, Anderson works as marketing manager at the Ski Apache Ski Resort in the nearby Sierra Blanca Mountains.

A Place to Get Hooked

Ruidoso

Antlers are a mainstay at Rustic Expressions, even though it's a furniture store. This is because antlers are used in a variety of ways to

★ ★

As the sign indicates, this store
in Ruidoso sells antler stuff.

both entice customers inside and then, once they're enticed, to con-
vince them they need something antlerish.

The store's sign is the giveaway. It's made of countless sets of antlers (countless because they're intertwined, snarled, and all tangled
together, making an accurate numerical assessment extremely difficult, if not impossible. Antlers, by their very nature, do not line up in
easily countable straight rows. They twist, turn, entangle, and otherwise make it difficult to determine exactly how many there, especially
when they're being used as a sign instead of simply lying side by side
on the ground).

Inside, the store offers antler lamps, antler tables, and antler sculptures. And as accents, they also sell antler candle holders, antler bookends, and antler ash trays. But they don't sell antler chairs.

Those who need something different in an outdoorsy way will find the store at 1500 Sudderth Drive/Highway 48 (phone number 575-257-7743). Go right on in; nobody's going to "horn" in on you. Just be careful what you lean against.

Mighty Steeds
Ruidoso Downs

Ruidoso Downs has sort of a dual personality; it is the name of both the town of Ruidoso Downs as well as Ruidoso Downs, the well-known race track. Since horse racing is such an integral part of the local history, it's not surprising that the Racehorse Hall of Fame is located here. And it's equally not surprising that Dave McGary's horse sculpture would be a dominant feature of the city's landscape.

The art work, titled *Free Spirits at Noisy Water,* stands at the Hubbard Museum of the American West and is composed of eight horses. But it's not the art itself that makes it a curiosity. Instead, it's the placement. The larger-than-life bronze horses are charging down a man-made hill and out onto the flatland at full gallop, making it so realistic that people have been observed shrinking back in alarm and even running away when they first notice them.

The horses represent seven different breeds—standardbred, Morgan, Arabian, American paint (with colt), Appaloosa, American quarter horse, and Thoroughbred. McGary created and installed the sculpture in 1995.

The museum is at 841 Highway 70 West. It pays homage to the American West and life in the early 1900s. Among the items on display is the extensive collection of Anne Stradling, an East Coast native with a passion for collecting things related to horses. It contains saddles, carriages, coaches, Indian artifacts, and fine art.

★ ★

The museum has an affiliation with the Smithsonian Institution which gives it access to major exhibitions rarely seen in towns as small as Ruidoso Downs. There's an admission fee at the museum but viewing the sculpture is free. For more information, log on to www .hubbardmuseum.org or call (575) 378-4142.

Kathy Whitworth Has Never Won Here
Tatum

It is not uncommon for the grand and glorious endeavor known as golf to be referred to as "cow pasture pool" or some other less-than-flattering designation. Despite that, the Cow Pasture Golf Tournament is highly unusual. Not only the fact that "cow pasture" is included in the official name, but the players, the course, the holes, the carts, the prizes, the clubs, and almost everything else commonly associated with the game of golf, in this case are, shall we say, highly individualistic.

As the name indicates, the tournament is played in a pasture. Prior to the event the greens keeper mows the grass down to about 3 inches high and places the cups and pins, which are actually plastic poles sticking out of five-gallon buckets set within a 10-foot circle. This would seem to make it easy to sink a putt except for the fact that the players can't use putters. They have to chip in.

Other deviations from the norm include the use of ATVs, jeeps, pickup trucks, and four-wheel-drive vehicles instead of golf carts, and a rather humane rule that declares if you can't find your own ball, find somebody else's and give it a whack because there are no lost-ball penalties.

The entry fees are $100 for each four-man team and all the money goes to Meals to You, a local charity. This madness in the meadow has been going on since 2004. Anyone interested in participating is urged to call Phil Jones at (575) 369-5005.

4

Southwest

There's no question that southwestern New Mexico is one of my favorite places. It is here that I encountered giant roadrunners, a golf hole more than two miles long, a 15-foot Indian head, and a sculpture that resembles a field of lightning rods. These are the things seekers of the unusual like myself dream about.

In this section of the state, I met folks who eat chiles for breakfast, lunch and dinner, and have recipes for a chile dessert. I gazed in wonder at the spot where a member of the Star Trek crew actually blasted off into outer space, and gaped in amazement at a solid rock replication of a toilet. I watched racing ducks waddle along the track and spent the night in a town named after an old television quiz show.

I winced when a balloon-snarfing rattlesnake sprang into action, visited the border town where a former enemy of America is now immortalized, had lunch in a small community that gets its name and livelihood from an all-time dessert favorite, and listened for voices from outer space in an area occupied by huge dish receptors that look like they could get a clear television signal from Mars.

And the people? They should all be appointed ambassadors of good will. They are kind, friendly, keenly observant, and always knew where the best hamburgers were made. And, most importantly, not one of them gave me a blank stare or a hint that maybe I should catch the next train out of town when I asked where to find the world's largest petrified meatball!

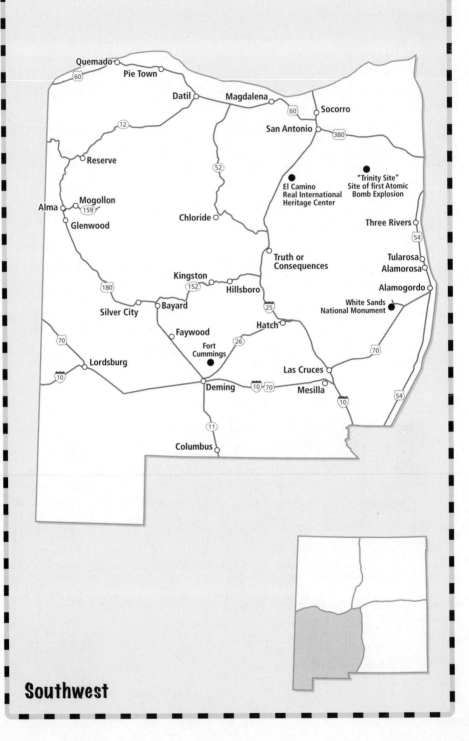

Southwest

★ ★

One Big Rusty Bird

Alamogordo

There's a big metal bird perched alongside the road on the outskirts of town, watching for potential customers. Or maybe it's waiting for a big metal critter to wander by so it can have lunch. Either way, it stands there because of a cooperative effort between a business firm and some eager teenagers.

Back in the 1990s, Basin Pipe and Metal needed something on the order of a road sign to make the firm more noticeable to those driving by, and easier to locate for those trying to find the place. And at the same time, it just so happened that students in a local high school welding class needed a project.

So the bargain was struck. The firm would provide the scrap metal and the high school students would provide the labor. The end result is a large roadrunner, skillfully crafted with smaller pieces of metal welded onto a steel frame to represent the feathers, and larger sheets used for the tail and beak. This one isn't as large as the one in Las Cruces, but it's about 8 feet tall and nearly 15 feet long so it definitely qualifies for membership in the Big Birds of America Club.

Because the icon sits out in the open, the metal has long since rusted so now it's sort of a light brownish umber instead of the usual blacks, whites, and grays commonly associated with the species. But

Students in a high school welding class created this huge roadrunner.

there's no doubt that it's a roadrunner, even though the bill is a bit droopy. Ornithologists and bird-watchers of the amateur sort will find this one north of Alamagordo on U.S. Highway 54, near where that roadway intersects with U.S. Highway 82.

Requiem for a Space Chimp
Alamogordo

Directly in front of the New Mexico Museum of Space History, a small metal plaque on a patch of grass marks the grave site of the world's first space chimp. His name was Ham.

His wild ride occurred on January 3, 1961. While strapped into a capsule that was attached to an 83-foot Redstone Rocket, Ham was blasted off from a launch pad at Cape Canaveral and moments later became the first free creature to travel into outer space. The contraption that bore him reached a top speed of 5,800 miles per hour, and took him 155 miles into the stratosphere before bringing him back to Earth 16.5 minutes later.

Ham (an acronym for "Holloman Aero Med") suffered no ill effects during his fantastic voyage. Nor did he reap any of the benefits bestowed on those who followed him into space. Astronaut John Glenn, for example, capitalized on his feat and earned a seat in the U.S. Senate. Astronaut Alan Shepherd got tons of publicity after hitting a golf ball on the moon. Ironically, however, Ham eventually did get to Washington, D.C., but as a resident of the National Zoo, where he lived for seventeen years. In 1981, at the urging of animal activists, he was moved to a zoological park in North Carolina where he spent the rest of his days. He died there on January 18, 1983, at the age of twenty-seven.

His remains were moved to Alamogordo in 1983 and given a hero's burial beneath the black marker on the front lawn of the International Space Hall of Fame, a part of the museum. The plaque reads: "Ham proved that mankind could live and work in space."

To visit Ham's grave site or any of the other features of the museum, coming from either the north or south, turn onto White Sands Boulevard. After about a mile (either direction), go east to the end of Indian Wells Road.

For information on how to pay tribute to the world's only astro-chimp, call (877) 333-6589 or log on to www.nmspacemuseum.org.

So Which One Is the Sunny Side of the Street?
Alamogordo

Tenth Street is a major thoroughfare that courses its way through downtown Alamogordo and into a residential area. It would not be very noteworthy except for the names of the streets that it intersects en route to its destination in the foothills.

The first few cross streets are named after states, including Delaware and Washington. Then, for some variety, they shift to international names like Cuba and Filipino. Then they switch to tree names like Maple and Elm. Next, it's presidents—Lincoln, Washington, and so on. And finally, apparently tired of making so many weighty decisions, the city fathers called upon the sun to not only heat and sustain the city, but also to serve as a namesake for the streets that go off it.

And so, for an 8-block stretch along Tenth, the streets have a sense of commonality because their names are Sunrise, Sunglow, Sunside, Sunset, Sundial, Sunshine, Sunbeam, and Sundown.

Oh, For Heaven's Snakes!
Alamogordo

Sure, everybody's seen footage of a rattlesnake snarfing down a mouse or baring its fangs at a television camera, but only a few can boast that they've actually watched a rattlesnake enter into mortal combat with a balloon. So here's the good news: Those who haven't but have always wanted to can fulfill their desires at Moore's Trading Post. And the even better news—it only costs a quarter.

★ ★

Tom Moore, the owner of this combination rattler hangout and antique/"junque" store, has been pitting snake against balloon for a couple of decades and, to date, the only casualties have been the air-inflated spheres.

It works thusly:

Customers who fork over two bits are given an uninflated balloon. Once the balloon is inflated, Moore attaches it to the end of a long pole and the fearless snake baiter thrusts the pole into a large pit filled with rattlers. They wave the balloons over the snakes until one of the reptiles lashes out and bites it, which creates a loud "pop" from the suddenly deflated balloon and, usually, loud shrieks from the person holding the other end of the pole.

"They strike because they sense the warm air inside the balloon and probably think it's something to eat," Moore explains. He has been running this operation for more than twenty years and has no idea of how many inflated pieces of rubber have met their doom in such fashion.

Moore has been handling snakes for twenty-seven years on his property at 215 US 82 about 3 miles east of Alamogordo (phone number 575-437-7116) and claims he's never been bitten. At two bits a pop, neither the owner nor the reptiles are getting rich. But at least the snakes have a pit to hiss in.

These Boots Weren't Made For Walkin'
Alamorosa

Let me tell ya, pardners, them folks what owns and operates the Boot Hill RV Resort sure know how to get a feller's attention. They sort of stomp right down on top of y'all and if ya ain't careful, they looks like they might squash ya flatter'n a polecat what's been run over by a pickup truck.

The signs promoting the sixty-unit facility are bitty little things, hardly no bigger'n a steer's rear end, so it'd be plumb easy to drive right on past 'em without payin' no never mind. But them cowboy boots, they sure ain't easy to miss because it looks like someone stole them right off the feet of Paul Bunyan when he was taking a little afternoon siesta down along the Rio Grande after a hard day of her-din' cows.

There's two of them big fellers, 8 feet tall and 6 feet long, a-sittin' on a couple of fence posts on US 54 between Tularosa and Alamo-gordo. And if that ain't enough to make yer eyes pop right out, they're also painted bright yeller and an even brighter red.

James Livens, the owner, found them lying around the yard when he bought the property. He gussied them up, put the new paint job on their fiberglass exteriors, installed some braces so he could attach them to the fence posts, and put 'em to work.

Wanna spend a night having nightmares about getting stomped on by a pair of size 165 EEEEE boots? The resort is at 1 Dog Ranch Road east of US 54. And iffen you cain't foller them big footprints, call the resort at (575) 439-6224 and ask for directions.

A Rocky End
Alma

One of the world's more unusual burial sites is a large rock located just east of Alma, a onetime bustling frontier town. It holds the remains of Sgt. James Cooney, who once discovered gold and silver deposits in the nearby Mogollon Mountains, and it's known, perhaps too obviously, as Cooney's Tomb.

After opening two mining camps, Cooney wrote in a letter to the *Grant County Herald* that he "had not seen a hostile Indian in this camp for three years." Less than two months later, he was killed by Victorio's Apaches. When his body was discovered by friends, they carved a large hollow into a boulder and put the corpse inside and then sealed it with ore from one of his mines.

The best way to get to Alma: Take U.S. Highway 180 northwest out of Silver City for about 60 miles. The best way to find the tomb: Turn west on Mineral Creek Road and go four miles.

★ ★

A Place to See Steel Stick Figures

Bayard

The Shrine of Our Lady of Guadalupe sits atop a hill and overlooks cars and pedestrians as they pass through town on US 180. Most people don't see it because they're en route to nearby Silver City, or because they don't happen to look up at just the right moment.

It features the familiar statue of the Blessed Virgin as she allegedly appeared to a farmer in Mexico in the 1800s. It would resemble many other shrines that dot New Mexico if it weren't for the Stations of the Cross.

The pathway leading to the shrine is lined with the Stations, but they are unlike so many others that use paintings and statuary to tell the story. These figures were shaped from steel rods. More than four decades ago, a local craftsman bent, twisted, and stretched the rods into the form of stick people and then attached them to wooden plaques and hung them along the path that goes to the top.

There's also a dirt road leading to the shrine, but it takes nerves of steel to drive it and, once there, it takes a belief in some higher power to get the vehicle turned around for the descent.

Father Gabriel Lopez, the pastor at nearby Our Lady of Fatima Catholic Church, started work on the shrine in 1962, but he died in a car accident before it was completed. Members of the parish finished the project and dedicated it to the priest as a way of preserving his memory.

Unfortunately, the memorial has fallen upon hard times. Some of the Stations have been vandalized, and the brick podium beneath the statue has become the target for graffiti applied by local spray painters.

Bayard is 5 miles east of Silver City on US 180.

But Are They Nice Elks?

Catron County

Catron County is the largest county in New Mexico. It is 76 miles wide and 91 miles long, which means it covers an area of more than 7,000 square miles or 4,414,720 acres, depending on how much of an impression one is trying to make.

Putting that in some sort of perspective, Catron County is larger than four American states—Connecticut (5,018 sq. mi.), Delaware (2,044), Hawaii (6,470), and Rhode Island (1,212)—and six American territories—Samoa (76.1), Guam (209), Midway Islands (2.1), Puerto Rico (3,539) Virgin Islands (136), and Wake Island (2.5).

And, to give it even more clout in the mine's-bigger-than-yours competition, Catron County is also larger (square miles-wise) than at least 41 independent nations, commonwealths, republics, and kingdoms. Some of them (with their dinky square mile totals listed in parentheses):

Andorra (180), Bahrain (267), Barbados (166), Brunei (2,226), the Federal Islamic Republic of the Comoros (719), Cyprus (3,572), Gambia (4,361), Grenada (133), Jamaica (4,244), Kiribati (332), Kuwait (6,880), and Lebanon (4,036).

Need more proof that this is one big whopping county? These countries also come up short against Catron County in the square mileage derby:

Liechtenstein (61.8), Luxembourg (999), Malta (122), Mauritius (788), Monaco (1.21), Qatar (4,416), San Marino (23.4), Seychelles (175), Swaziland (6,704), Trinidad and Tobago (1,980), and Vanuatu (4,707).

But don't expect any bullying talk from the state's largest county because there's an offsetting factor:

Forestland covers about half the county and the last census counted only 3,543 full-time human residents, so Catron is probably the only county in the world that has more elk than people. On the

★ ★

other hand, it also means that every human inhabitant has about two square miles all to themselves. And the people there are rarely bothered by tourists looking for a sushi bar.

One Way to Derail the Hail
Chloride

Only a very few of the buildings erected here during this town's boom days are still standing. Once, back in the 1890s, an estimated 3,000 people lived here, drawn by the lure of silver deposits in the nearby hills. But the price of silver dropped, the mother lodes began running out, and the residents started moving away.

One who stayed, at least temporarily, was Austin Crawford, a Scottish immigrant who arrived in the area around 1910. He worked as a stonemason, mining investor, and builder but his focus changed when he got religion around 1920. Shortly after that, Crawford began telling the townspeople that he had been talking with God, and that God had warned him to expect a monstrous hailstorm that would destroy the town and all the sinners living in it.

Although he claimed to have direct contact with the heavens, Crawford apparently decided to hedge his bet by building a hail-storm-proof structure. Using rocks from a creek and other miscellaneous building supplies, he constructed a three-room house with a roof pitched so steep that the hailstones would merely bounce off it without doing any damage.

The storm never came. According to historians, Crawford left Chloride about five years later and allegedly died in an asylum. But his anti-hail house still stands. It has three rooms, none of them connected, and each room has its own basement area that is also unconnected to the others.

Chloride is just off Highway 52, about 30 miles northwest of Truth or Consequences and two miles southwest of Winston on Forest Road 226.

The Day Pancho Rode into Town
Columbus

This town has the rather dubious distinction of being a National Historic Site because it was the scene of the last foreign invasion of the continental United States by a military force.

Columbus, originally settled in the 1890s, was a bustling border community on March 9, 1916, when Francisco "Pancho" Villa, the Mexican revolutionary general, led an army of 800 on a predawn raid across the border. The invaders torched homes, looted guns and ammunition, and killed eighteen Americans. The town then became the launching site for the historic eleven-month Punitive Expedition into Mexico, led by Gen. John "Black Jack" Pershing.

Ironically, Villa's cause was initially supported by the United States. But the bandit leader felt betrayed by Washington and began attacking Americans in Mexico. When the situation grew worse, historians say, Villa felt the incursion into Columbus was justified.

The raid was a disaster for Villa, however. An army cavalry unit repulsed the invaders and sent them scurrying back into Mexico with heavy losses. Days later, President Woodrow Wilson sent 10,000 soldiers under Pershing's command to invade Mexico and capture Villa. They never did. He eventually negotiated peace and retired. There was, however, a beneficial side effect to the incursion—the expedition proved fruitful as a training ground for air and motorized vehicle transportation used by the American military in World War I.

Fortunately, time heals all wounds. Columbus now observes the invasion with an annual fiesta in Pancho Villa State Park, located right in the heart of the city and probably the only park in the nation to be named after a former enemy. Visitors may also tour the museum inside the old Columbus Railroad Depot where a variety of relics from Villa's time are on display. Columbus is located 35 miles south of Deming on Highway 11.

★ ★

A Wee Bit of Education

Datil

What is probably the world's smallest public library could also be the world's loneliest public library.

The Baldwin Cabin Public Library is housed in an old ranger cabin owned by the National Forest Service. The building is typically small and isolated. It keeps a silent watch over a wooded area about 6 miles west of Datil on U.S. Highway 60 with only an old barn for company.

But on Wednesdays and Saturdays, the library comes alive because those are the days it is open, from 10:00 in the morning until 2:00 in the afternoon. On other days, a note hanging on the door advises readers of the hours and then adds, "When the weather is bad and the roads are worse, it is a good possibility that the library will be closed."

(Those who want to make sure it's open may call 505-772-5230. Of course, the librarians will be really impressed if you tell them you

The public library at Datil is housed in
a lonely old forest ranger station.

already know that the correct pronunciation of Datil is "DAT-uhl." It's that way even though the name came from Spanish settlers who thought the seed pods of the ubiquitous yucca plants resembled dates, and the Spanish word for "date" is "datil" and because it's Spanish it should be pronounced "da-TEEL.")

Despite the library's lack of size, librarian Diane Olmstead says the facility offers more than 9,000 volumes to area students, be they young or old. Most of the books were donated. So were most of the DVDs and videos.

And the nice thing about being out there in the middle of the forest is that nobody tells you to be quiet. It already has enough of that.

The Morley Monument

Datil

A couple of miles west of the Baldwin Cabin Library, on the opposite side of the road, a large stone monolith juts up out of the ground in the most unlikely of places—a pasture. This could cause some speculation that it may have been left there eons ago by aliens as a homing device for other UFO pilots.

But although that's an interesting scenario, it has nothing to do with the real reason that a 10-foot-tall granite cylinder is sticking up out of a pasture. The real reason is that it's a tribute to the Morley family, pioneers whose roots go back to the late 1800s. A plaque on the memorial reads: "To the memory of William Raymond Morley. Born Sept. 15, 1846. Died January 3, 1883. In whom were combined courage, loyalty, love and honor; every manly virtue and all noble qualities of heart. This monument is erected by his friends."

Four large rocks form a semicircle around the monolith and bronze plaques attached to each memorialize other family members. Sylvanus Griswold Morley was an archaeologist and author; William Raymond Morley IV was killed on Iwo Jima during World War II; William Raymond Morley Jr. was inducted into both football and cowboy halls of fame; and William Morley Warren was chairman of the

★ ★

A granite monument in a pasture pays tribute to a pioneer New Mexican family.

world's largest tin producer with mines in Burma, Thailand, Malaysia, and Australia.

Although she's not included in the memorial, Agnes Morley Cleaveland, William Raymond Morley's daughter, achieved a degree of fame when she wrote a book titled *No Life for a Lady*, about growing up in a pioneer family during the 1880s.

Unfortunately for curiosity seekers, the monument is on private land posted with "No Trespassing" signs so it's best to view it from the road.

Running Ducks, Flying Tortillas, and Speedy Outhouses

Deming

So what's a city to do when it's suddenly faced with economic disaster?

Turn the situation over to the ducks, of course.

Deming did, and it worked wonders.

In the late 1970s a shirt factory that had been a major employer in Deming for several years shut down, putting the city in a bit of a crisis mode. A group of businessmen held discussions on how to counteract the factory's demise and came up with (and this is for real, folks) duck races. Get some ducks, build some racing pens, and turn 'em loose. Ducky. Just ducky.

The first one was held in 1980 and it was a triumph beyond anyone's expectations, attracting not only duck-racing fans but also national and international media attention.

Athletic ducks take center stage
once every year in Deming.

And in an ending that could happen only in Deming, the second-place finisher in the first Great American Duck Race was (drum roll, please) Robert Duck, a duck racer from Bosque Farms, New Mexico. Duck's ducks went on to win the event for several years after that before ducking out of the competition.

As the event grew in popularity, it also grew in size. The first races were for running ducks only, but now there's also a competition for swimming ducks that paddle in water-filled lanes just like Olympians except they don't have to wear Speedos.

In addition, the annual festivities now include the Great American Tortilla Toss, plus the Outhouse Races in which three-person teams careen through the streets on vehicles designed to look like what used to be blushingly referred to as "the little house behind the big house."

The Tournament of Ducks Parade down Gold Street opens the two-day affair. Then the city stages the Great American Duck Royalty Pageant in which contestants in various age groups waddle around the stage while dressed like ducks. And the person in charge of the whole thing is called (get ready for this one, folks) the Quackmaster.

Daffy and Donald groupies can acquire more information by logging on to www.demingduckrace.com or by calling (888) 345-1125. Just don't make any wisequacks.

Do-It-Yourself Ghosting
Deming

Here's the peculiar thing about ghost towns: They rarely, if ever, show up in the "For Sale" section of the classified ads for real estate. So when Randy and Sally McCowan faced that situation after migrating to Luna County from California in 1995, they did the next best thing: They built their own.

Shortly after settling into their new surroundings, the couple envisioned the creation of a little town as it would have appeared a century ago. When they got it totally envisioned, Randy went to work.

He not only built the town, which he named Olmesquite, but also compiled a fake history of the place, basing it primarily on his own forebears.

His wild and woolly tale of origin lists Civil War veteran John McCowan, his fictitious great-grandfather, as the founder of Olmesquite and other make-believe relatives as the settlers who populated his community. He introduces cowpokes, saloonkeepers, merchants, prostitutes, lawmen, and outlaws in the two-page narration, all of which is a product of McCowan's fertile mind. Part of it reads:

"By 1892, the town consisted of a cafe, three saloons, laundry and bath, boarding house, land office, livery, blacksmith shop, bakery, jail and The House. One day four ladies came to town in a wagon and started a business in an old abandoned adobe house. From that day on, their place was just called The House."

According to his version of history, Olmesquite was a swingin' place until it became a ghost town when the last store closed in 1920. Now it's back, but not as a commercial venture because McCowan built it for fun and to satisfy his long-held personal desire.

Olmesquite, located seven miles southwest of Deming, is not a place where you can just drop in and say "howdy" because McCowan wants to be there to meet you, greet you, and show you around. However, those who share his enthusiasm for times gone by can easily get a tour by looking up his number in the Deming phone book and contacting him.

A Mighty Flush
Faywood

There are times when something off in the distance looks so real that it's almost like seeing a mirage. This happens northwest of Deming, when the City of Rocks State Park pops into view and takes on the appearance of a major city rising up in the middle of nowhere.

It's not a real city, of course. The things that look like skyscrapers are actually rocks. Big rocks. Really big rocks. But from a couple of

★ ★

miles away, they strongly resemble a cityscape, especially to cartoon fans who once watched Fred Flintstone and Barney Rubble cavort around Bedrock.

For those who prefer a more realistic explanation, the rocks are all volcanic deposits with such technical names as basalt, andresite, and rhyolite, and they were spewed up from the inner earth more than thirty million years ago. The big, really big, rocks were formed when the lava cooled and solidified, then erosion over ensuing years sculpted the forms as they appear today.

And when they got done hardening, congealing and eroding, the rocks took on some pretty odd shapes. One looks like a giant mushroom. Others resemble abstract couples in fond embrace, and several have features that appear to be human faces, particularly when the lighting is just right.

But the centerpiece that draws the most attention is right next to the park entrance. Viewed from any angle, it appears to be a giant toilet.

The place to go is this toilet-shaped
rock in City of Rocks State Park.

The City of Rocks State Park, established in May 1952, encompasses a square mile in the Chihuahuan Desert region at an elevation of 5,200 feet. To get there, take US 180 north out of Deming for 23 miles, turn east on Highway 61 and drive about 3 miles to the site. Facilities include camp sites, hiking trails, picnic areas and a desert botanical garden. For information about the park, visit www.emnrd .state.nm.us/PRD/cityrocks.htm or call the park manager at (505) 536-2800.

So How Did They Spell "Soldierette"?
Fort Cummings

Way back in 1866, an ex-slave walked into an army recruiting office in Missouri, signed up, and then left the office as William Cathey, a member of the Buffalo Soldiers, a nickname given to the all-black regiments by Indians because of the members' curly black hair and fighting ability.

Cathey, probably sixteen at the time, was readily accepted. Jobs were scarce and the army assured the young recruits that they'd be well fed, have good medical benefits, and be paid regularly. Physical exams weren't required because the army was badly in need of soldiers to fight on the western frontier. So recruits were checked only to see if they could march and shoot.

So day after day, Private Cathey stood guard, drilled, marched, and stood ready to fire the musket when the occasion demanded it, while hiding a secret that would have meant immediate discharge from the service.

Eventually, however, the secret came out. William Cathey, the soldier, was actually Cathay Williams, a young woman who had enlisted because she needed a job. Although it was not unusual for women to conceal their gender and enlist in the military at the time—several had disguised themselves as men and served on both sides during the Civil War—Cathay Williams was the only documented female Buffalo Soldier.

★ ★

But in 1868, while stationed at Fort Cummings, Williams grew tired of military life, so she went to the post infirmary and revealed her true identity rather than serve the final year of her enlistment. Understandably, this did not sit well with the men in her outfit who had marched, dined, and slept beside her. She was mustered out but her discharge papers listed her as "he."

Fort Cummings has long been abandoned. The ruins, in Luna County near Deming, are maintained by the Bureau of Land Management.

The Cats Don't Actually Use It
Glenwood

It's called the Catwalk, but cats are smart enough not to use it. And despite the name, it was never meant for felines. Humans constructed it and humans still use it.

The original Catwalk was built in the 1890s to follow a pipeline that delivered water up Whitewater Canyon to the mining town of Graham. In frontier days the area was a hideout for the likes of Butch Cassidy and Victorio's Apache warriors.

The pipe, laid along Whitewater River, was a mere 18 inches in diameter, so those who worked on it needed nerves of steel and the balance of a cat, hence the name.

Now it's called the Catwalk National Scenic Trail, and hikers no longer have to straddle the pipeline because there's a walkway with four-foot metal sides running over the top. But even with that precaution, the walk across it can create some heavy breathing and hard swallowing. The Catwalk is attached to the rock wall 25 to 30 feet above the stream in a canyon so narrow that hikers can almost touch both sides, so walking across it gives the hikers a sense that they're suspended in mid-air.

And while tromping across the creaking metal grates, visitors invariably look down, directly into the swiftly running water below. Besides that, it's poorly lit. The walls are so steep and narrow that the sun's rays don't reach the walkway until high noon in the summer and rarely, if ever, during the winter.

The National Forest Service built the metal walkway in the 1960s, and it withstands the elements very well. But the trail leading to it has to be rebuilt occasionally due to flooding.

The Catwalk is in the Gila National Forest about 5 miles northeast of Glenwood on Highway 174/Catwalk Road. For more information, see the forest website at www2.srs.fs.fed.us/r3/gila/recreation/attractions.

Do You Feel the Burn?
Hatch

There are two items the citizens of Hatch are quick to point out when a stranger stops by to ask about chile. First, the word is spelled "chile." Never, never, never *ever* "chili." Second, they don't grow the most chiles in the world here. But those they do grow are the world's best. Ask any resident.

Although area agrarians also other produce such foodstuffs as onions, potatoes, cabbage, wheat, and pecans, the chile is what gives Hatch so much notoriety that it can proudly proclaim itself "the chile capital of the world" without being challenged.

The claim is the reason behind the annual Hatch Chile Festival, held on the Labor Day weekend and featuring the coronation of a Chile Queen, chile cook-offs, and chile ristra-making contests. (Ristras are arrangements of dried chile peppers.) It's also why the streets are lined with chile banners attached to street lights and utility poles.

The community's dedication to the chile is perhaps best exemplified at the Hatch Chile Express, a small store located at 622 Franklin (Highway 26). It sells chile-related things. Lots of chile-related things. Like chile soap, chile tee shirts, and chile banks, clocks, magnets, cups, coasters, plates, trays, socks, key chains, nightlights, place mats, and cookie jars.

★ ★

Those Chiles Are Definitely Not Chilly

The chile is New Mexico's official state vegetable, which is logical because this state grows more chiles than any of the other forty-nine. The chile arrived here as early as 1598, accompanied by Spanish explorers. It comes in two colors but both colors are from the same plant. The green chile is fresh off the plant; the reds have been allowed to ripen. As a result New Mexico also has an "official state question": "Red or green?"

Incidentally, the fire that lurks within the chile and is released upon consumption by an unwary human is not caused by the chile itself. It's those sneaky little seeds that turn your belly into a raging inferno where Rolaids go to die.

They also sell chile jellies that combine blueberry, peach, mango, papaya, raspberry, and pineapple flavors with chiles. They sell chile wind chimes, chile wind socks, pens, bulletin boards, salad-dressing dispensers, aprons, candle holders, barbecue sauce, salsa, ball caps, and a chile fish lure that tells the buyer to cast the chile into the water so the fish can swallow it, and then when it comes to the surface to spit out the hot seeds, the fisherman can scoop it up with the provided chile net.

And, of course, they also sell chiles.

Hatch is 36 miles north of Las Cruces and 186 miles south of Albuquerque off I-25. Need more information on where to get a case of good ol' homegrown heartburn? Log onto www.villageofhatch.org or call (505) 267-5050.

One of Those "Nice Try" Situations

Hillsboro

In its prime Hillsboro was a fairly good-sized town of about 1,200 because it was a center for mining activity. It sprang up around 1877 when three prospectors found gold deposits in the surrounding hills. But the hills apparently had nothing to do with naming the town. One story says the prospectors drew the name from a hat. Another says it was named Hillsborough in honor of one prospector's hometown in Ohio. Following the time-honored American tradition of shortening things, it eventually became just Hillsboro.

Because of its prominence as a mining town, the town was named the county seat for Sierra County in 1884. But after producing more than $6 million in gold and silver, the area mines went belly up and the population dwindled to such an extent that in 1936, the county seat was moved to Hot Springs, (now Truth or Consequences) some 32 miles to the northeast.

All the files and records were removed from the courthouse in Hillsboro and transferred to the new one in Hot Springs. Understandably, this did not sit well with those who remained in Hillsboro, so they devised a plan to bring the county seat back. And so one night in 1936, several residents of Hillsboro staged a midnight raid on Hot Springs, grabbed all the important documents, and hauled them back to where the raiders figured they rightfully belonged.

Understandably, again, this did not sit well with the folks in Hot Springs. They called in the authorities and the sheriff went over to Hillsboro the next day, retrieved the files and records, and lugged them back to Hot Springs.

Later, after accepting the finality of it all, Hillsboro's town leaders decided that since they were no longer the county seat, there was little reason to keep the courthouse. So they tore it down and sold it off, brick by brick.

★ ★

To get there, take exit 68 off Interstate 25 and go about 18 miles west on Highway 152. Hillsboro has become an off-the-beaten-path arts community with a current population of about 150.

There's Art In Those Logs
Las Cruces

Peter Wolf Toth arrived in Las Cruces in the mid-1980s, determined to add one of his massive artworks to the city's landscape. He told the city fathers that he'd do the project for nothing. All he asked was that they provide him with a log and a place to put his sculpture once it was completed.

Peter Wolf Toth carved an Indian head in all
50 states, including this one in Las Cruces.

★ ★

When he finished about four months later, he left behind a 20-foot Indian head in a city park. Twenty years later, it's still performing sentry duty while serving as a photo opportunity.

The sculpture is part of the series Toth called "The Trail of the Whispering Giants." After his family fled Communist-controlled Hungary in the 1960s and settled in Ohio, he developed a passion for the history of American Indians and what he considered unjust treatment accorded them by settlers and the government. So he set out on a mission of protest that would involve carving at least one huge Indian head in all fifty states. He started in California and then crisscrossed the country, spending four to six months on each sculpture.

His New Mexico project, carved from a pine log, stands in a public park on Solano Drive between North Main and Madrid. It was the fifty-seventh in his series (some states got more than one and he also created huge heads in several Canadian provinces). When each carving was finished, Toth applied about one hundred coats of preservative to make sure it withstood the elements.

The mission was a success, from the standpoint of making a statement in every state. He once told a newspaper reporter, "I study the Indians of the area, then visualize an Indian within the log. It is a composite of all the native people of the state."

New Mexican sculpture fans on a limited travel budget will also find Toth's works in Winslow, Arizona; Troy, Kansas; Broken Bow, Oklahoma; Murray, Utah; and Texarkana, Texas. His final effort, completed in 1988, stands on the North Shore of Oahu, Hawaii. There's no charge for viewing any of them.

A Very Large Beep Beeper
Las Cruces

Since the roadrunner is New Mexico's Official State Bird, it's only logical that New Mexico should be the home of the world's largest roadrunner. And so it is.

The world's largest roadrunner near
Las Cruces was rescued from a landfill.

The humungous creature peers down on Las Cruces from atop a
mesa at a rest stop on the south side of Interstate 10 on the western
edge of the city. What makes it more of an oddity is that it is not
only impressive, it is not only huge, but also a major recycling project.

The big bird is about 15 feet tall and 30 feet long. The framework
is steel reinforcing rod, and the body is stuffed with trash that was
salvaged from an old landfill where the bird once resided. When the
landfill closed in 2000, the city rescued the bird and immediately
moved it to its present site.

Old and well-used white athletic shoes were inserted into the bottom of the frame to compose the bird's pale underbelly. The top,
neck, wings, and tail were done with whatever else Olin S. Calk, the
creator, could salvage from the rubbish heaps. This includes discarded
electric fans, used tires, computers, automobile parts, sticks, stones,

and clothing. And old bicycle parts, raggedy tennis shoes, typewriter keyboards, kitchen utensils, and a variety of things that don't resemble things found on this earth.

The beak looks like it was fashioned either from tin buckets that were flattened and reshaped, or pieces of rusted sheet metal. The eyes were originally mini-hubcaps, the tail feathers are made of sheet metal, and the feet were constructed by wrapping wire around hunks of leather.

This majestic state symbol may be viewed by taking the rest stop exit off Interstate 10 between mile markers 134 and 135. It's only accessible to eastbound traffic.

Lost among the Veggies
Las Cruces

The Mesilla Valley Maze is one cornfield you have to see to believe. The only problem is that in order to see it, you have to stand at least 150 feet tall or own a light aircraft, glider, or helicopter because it's one of those things best viewed from far above.

It's a joint venture between New Mexico State University's Survey Department and the Lyles Family Farms, and it covers nine acres. The process begins in January, when professors, students, and farmers draw up a pencil sketch that represents the coming year's endeavor. Next, the sketch goes to the department heads of the university's Survey-Engineering Program, who team with a select group of students to digitize the drawing and calculate the ground coordinates for the global positioning satellites.

The corn is planted the first week in July, and when it grows to about 2 feet, the creator's stake out the design. Then they use a small farm tractor mounted with special GPS equipment to cut the maze. Later, the team's official photographer flies over the cornfield to take the official photograph.

Each maze has a specific theme such as "Voyage of Discovery," "Lost in the Old West," and "Spirit of the West," which featured a

huge windmill and waterfall. "Millennium Moo" was a giant cow and "Country Corn" displayed an eight-acre scarecrow.

Once all the legwork is done, the maze is opened to the public, in conjunction with hayrides, face painting, pumpkin patches, and picnics. When adventurers have had all the fun they can stand, the cornfield is plowed under to get ready for the next year's maze.

The farm and cornfield are at 3855 West Picacho Road. Take exit 139 off I-10 and go north on Motel Boulevard to Picacho. Turn left. For more information, log onto www.mesillavalleymaze.com or call (575) 526-1919.

A Watered-Down Space Voyage
Las Cruces

The Space Mural Museum is curious for several reasons. One is the size of the mural itself. It's almost 30 feet high and is wrapped around the 1.2 million-gallon water tank that sits out in the back- yard. Another is the collection of space artifacts, including many from people involved in the space program. And finally, the pond where the koi fish live is shaped like a spaceship.

And besides that, the landscape is dotted with rockets and other items used to send humans and cargo into outer space.

But what makes the place even more unusual is that there's no admission charge. Visitors can wander around, look at rocket replicas, have their pictures taken next to a space suit, and gaze at more than 2,500 space-related photographs, and it's all free. Of course, if they so choose, visitors may also spend some time browsing around in the gift shop where things aren't free.

Owner Louis Gariano wrote to almost 200 astronauts, pilots, launch pad technicians, and many others associated with the aero- space industry, asking for items he could display in his museum. He started the project in the early 1990s and is still adding to his collec- tion. Most of the people he contacted responded with such artifacts as space gloves, space helmets, autographs, and spacecraft models.

The mural was originally painted in 1992 by Royce Vann and then retouched by Josh Flores and Peter Knapp in 2004. It depicts spacemen, spaceships, space satellites, and space rockets. It's located at 12450 Highway 70 East, 10 miles northeast of Las Cruces on U.S. Highway 70, north of Mesilla Park. For information, log on to www.zianet.com/spacemurals or call (575) 382-0977.

That's A Lotta Enchilada
Las Cruces

Worried about what to do when 200 unexpected guests drop in for dinner?

Perhaps this will ease your mind. It's the recipe they use here every year to create the world's largest enchilada:

Take 750 pounds of stone-ground corn and mix it with a big bucket of water to make the masa. While heating 175 gallons of vegetable oil to cook the enchilada, prepare 75 gallons of red chile sauce, grate 175 pounds of cheese, and chop 60 pounds of onions.

Next, place the dough on top of a carrying tray and use a huge press to flatten it. Then get 14 big guys to help carry the tortilla to the cooking vat where the oil has been heated to 550 degrees, and plop it in. (Note: According to the directions given on the Web site, "this is a difficult procedure.")

When it's done cooking, have the 14 men haul the tortilla to the serving plate and carefully lay it out. (The Web site notes that "this is another one of our difficult procedures.") Next, spread the chile sauce, cheese, and onions over the surface. Then roll it up and serve.

The entire process, from mixing the ground corn to slathering on the chile sauce, takes about two and one-half hours.

★ ★

They go through this cooking ritual every September as part of the Whole Enchilada Fiesta, a three-day event that also includes parades, races, and dancing. The tortilla measures up to 12 feet across and about 2 inches high before the goodies are added, and it's about a foot thick when everything gets rolled up inside. The final step comes when the giant tummy-filler is distributed among those who come to watch and drool.

For more information on how to fix lunch for a small army, log on to www.enchiladafiesta.com or call (575) 524-7824.

But You Don't Dare Call 'Em Pink Ladies
Las Cruces

On September 29, 2007, the large men and swift runners who were playing for the New Mexico State University football team took the field for a game against the equally huge men but not quite as swift runners who represented the University of Arkansas/Pine Bluff.

The NMSU Aggies were wearing pink socks.

They also had pink ribbons attached to their helmets.

And their coaches were clad in pink golf shirts.

The playing field was painted with large pink ribbon stencils, members of the university's marching band also were clad in pink, and the motto for the game was, "Aggies Are Tough Enough to Wear Pink."

But nobody in the stadium, including the players from the opposing team, made any cute remarks about their color selections. It was all for a good cause.

The unusual (for football games) color scheme was part of a promotion designed to raise money for breast-cancer research, and the players readily agreed because head coach Hal Mumme's wife, June, was a victim of the disease. She survived and subsequently became active in the cause during her husband's coaching stops at Valdosta State (Ga.), Kentucky, and Southeastern Louisiana. The 2007 season was her husband's third year at New Mexico State.

University officials agreed to pick up the tab for most of the costs associated with the game promotion, but the legwork was done by organizers working behind the scenes. All the funds generated went toward cancer research in New Mexico.

And sometimes good deeds are rewarded. Because of the pink socks, or perhaps in spite of them, the Aggies won the game, 20–17.

Avon Calling . . . and Calling . . . and Calling
Lordsburg

The collection of old stuff and historically important stuff gathered under the roof of the Lordsburg–Hidalgo County Museum is, by museum standards, relatively standard. Artifacts from the Korean, Vietnam, Desert Storm, and both World Wars are on display in the Military Room. The Mining Room highlights the area's economic mainstay. The Prisoner of War Room contains one of the most complete collections of POW history and memorabilia in existence.

The Johnson Photo Room is a comprehensive pictorial history of Lordsburg from the 1800s to the present.

Many of the displays line the perimeter of a large area known as the Great Room, where visitors may study railroad history as reflected in a diorama of Rodeo, New Mexico, or look at photos of Charles Lindbergh taken when he landed here to help dedicate the local airport in 1927.

Elsewhere, the museum boasts an arrowhead collection, mineral and rock collection and the ubiquitous

Avon bottles of all shapes and sizes grace the shelves of a museum in Lordsburg.

assortment of antique tools. And the Hidalgo County Cattle Growers Association Hall of Fame.

But then there's the Bottle Room, a simple little area that elevates the museum into the curiosity category.

Tucked into a small space behind the old typewriters, the room contains an estimated 1,500 bottles and jars that once held Avon products. Some are in the shape of frogs and trains, some look like glass cars and clocks, and others were cast to look like dolls and ducks.

The shelves are lined with glass and ceramic beer steins, pipes, and horses that once contained products designed to make women (and perhaps some men) look younger and more beautiful. The entire collection was donated by Lyne Lesly-Hassenger, who rang doorbells and uttered the familiar "Avon calling" greeting in and around the community for more than four decades.

The museum is at 708 East Second Street. Take exit 22 off I-10, go north on Main Street, and then turn right on Second. The phone is (575) 542-9086. Go and see the many faces of beauty.

One Way to Reduce Mayhem
Lordsburg

Shakespeare was once a mining boomtown with a population of more than 3,000, but those days are gone and it's probably for the best, considering its rather colorful, but violent, history.

It was not a typical frontier town. It had twenty-three saloons but not a single church, newspaper, or school. It was named after the English writer. And the residents never elected a town marshal or city council because they dealt with lawbreakers in frontier fashion. For example, Russian Bill and Sandy King were both hanged in the dining room of the Butterfield Stage Office because there weren't any trees in town. Bill's crime was cheating on a mining claim; King got his for being "a darned nuisance."

Johnny Ringo, a contemporary of the men involved in the infamous gunfight at the OK Corral in Tombstone, Arizona, allegedly bought his last pair of boots here before he was gunned down. And Beanbelly Smith made his niche in history when he shot and killed another man during an argument over who was going to get the last egg for breakfast in a local hotel.

Although it was unwritten, the locals did adhere to one rule: If you shot someone in Shakespeare, you had to bury him. The rule, coupled with the fact that the ground around the community was primarily rock, held the murder/"self-defense" rate to a minimum.

When the silver boom ended, Shakespeare's population underwent a rapid decline. Worried about their investments, landowners salted nearby hills with low-grade diamonds in the hope that it would bring the fortune hunters back. It didn't work. By the early 1930s everybody was gone. The property has been privately owned since 1935 and is open to the public only once or twice each month.

Shakespeare is 2.5 miles southwest of Lordsburg off Main Street. Call (575) 542-9034 for tour times and admission prices.

A Face in the Rocks

Magdalena

Many towns can only trace the histories of how their towns were named back a couple of centuries at best, but Magdalena has been Magdalena for almost 500 years. The community was given the name in 1540 when a Spanish soldier saw what he thought was the face of Mary Magdalene on the side of a mountain that overlooks the town.

Originally, it was a wild and woolly place inhabited by outlaws, gamblers, and other ne'er-do-wells. But, although the supposed face was shaped by rocks, shadows, and bushes, the mountain became somewhat of a religious place of refuge during the lawless years when the town was overrun by bars, houses of ill repute, and undesirable persons.

Over the centuries, the face on the mountain has been altered so drastically by time and the elements that only a very few know where

it is, and it takes some serious squinting and a fairly vivid imagination to recognize it. But the town name remains the same.

Magdalena, a small community of fewer than 1,000 residents located at the intersections of US 60 and Highway 169, has a theatrical company and arts council. There's also a walking tour that takes visitors to a variety of historic buildings, including the old railroad station that now houses City Hall, and the Salome General Store that has been open since 1910.

The ghost town of Kelly sits about three miles south of Magdalena. It once had a population of more than 3,000 when the mines and smelter were operational. When they left, so did the people. Most of the town is in ruins, but a small church still holds services once a year.

Capitalizing on The Kid
Mesilla

In 1881 Billy the Kid was captured here, charged with murder, tried, and found guilty. The trial was held in the local courthouse and the young outlaw was sentenced to hang. But, as he did on several other occasions, Billy escaped and spared himself the ignominy of being strung up, much to the delight of the dime novelists, who were making a decent living at the time by telling his story to those gullible easterners.

The courthouse had already achieved some degree of fame before that incident, having served as the capitol of Arizona and New Mexico when they were still lumped together as the Arizona Territory. Built around 1840, the building housed a store until after the Civil War, when it was converted into the courthouse and was used in that capacity until 1882. Later, it became a coal and feed storage site, carpenter shop, cantina, and pool hall. Still later, it was placed on the National Historic Register.

And now it's a souvenir shop named, naturally, the Billy the Kid Gift Shop. And it sells Billy the Kid items like Billy the Kid cups and

Billy the Kid bandannas. For a quarter visitors can get their fortune told by a mechanized Billy the Kid. For another quarter they can buy Billy the Kid bubble gum. The shop also sells several items that have no connection to Billy.

Need a key chain to fill out your Billy the Kid collection? You'll probably find one in "his" gift shop at 2385 Calle de Guadalupe on the town plaza. To reach Mesilla, take exit 140 off I-10, and go 1 mile south on Highway 28. To reach the courthouse, turn west on Calle de Santiago, and then in 2 blocks, go south on Calle de Guadalupe. Better call (505) 523-5561 first to make sure they have one in stock.

There's Something Weird Going On Here
Mesilla

Why weren't starships used during the construction of the Great Pyramid? How could a dentist accurately describe starships in 1882? Why isn't John Newbrough recognized as a visionary like his contemporaries?

The literature extolling the virtues of a visit to the Shalam Colony and Oahspe Mystery Museum claims the museum holds the answers. But like so many promises of complete enlightenment, visitors will find that the truth is pretty much a matter of interpretation.

The museum is dedicated to the life of Dr. John Ballou Newbrough, who, according to the brochures, was "the visionary who out-visioned Jules Verne and H. G. Wells." He was a prominent New York dentist who came to New Mexico in the 1880s and founded Shalam County in the desert north of Las Cruces. He called it a communitarian village and the residents were known as "Faithists." They were vegetarians and believed their purpose on earth was to collectively raise and educate homeless infants as a gradual remedy to world poverty.

Newbrough also wrote *Oahspe,* a book that his followers claim was channeled to him through his typewriter. A portion of it reads:

"One morning, I accidentally looked out of the window and beheld the line of light that rested on my hands extending heavenward like a telegraph wire to the sky. Over my head were three pairs of hands, fully materialized, behind me stood another Angel with her hands on my shoulders. My looking did not disturb the scene; my hands kept right on printing . . . printing."

The colony was abandoned in 1907, sixteen years after the death of its founder. But the questions and the claims linger in the small museum at 1910 Calle de Parian, to the west off Highway 28, inside the Old Tortilla Factory Shops. For hours and details, call (575) 524-9830.

Don't Mess with the Politicos
Mesilla

The first settlers came here after the Treaty of Guadalupe Hidalgo ended the Mexican-American War in 1848. It was a logical selection because both the Chihuahua-to-Santa Fe and the San Antonio-to-San Diego trails crossed through the community so it was a a bustling place. By 1858, Mesilla had gone from a struggling colony to the largest town between San Antonio and San Diego.

But those who lived there soon discovered they were in a no-man's land because both the United States and Mexico claimed the area due to a boundary dispute, so the residents weren't sure if they were American or Mexican.

After that issue was settled by the Gadsden Purchase in 1854, the city incorporated and political parties formed, which created some pretty heated rivalries, even by the standards of that time.

The discord came to a head on August 27, 1871, when members of both the Democratic and Republican Parties announced rallies on the plaza. They agreed to meet in separate areas. The whiskey flowed freely, and when the meetings ended, both groups staged processions around the plaza. Inevitably, they met.

Gunfire and fistfights followed. Nine men were killed and as many fifty wounded. Troops from nearby Fort Selden were called in to quell the mayhem, and they had to stay in town for three nights before order was restored. There was no judge in the district so the townspeople summoned one from another district to conduct an investigation.

After three days the jurist decided the situation was too dangerous so he left town. No further action was ever taken and no one was ever convicted of anything.

The plaza where it all happened is in the heart of downtown Mesilla, between Calle de Parian and Calle de Santiago.

Don't Mess with the Flag, Either

Mesilla

The Gadsden Purchase was signed on the Mesilla Plaza and was consummated when troops from Fort Fillmore raised an American flag over the site in 1854. Because of its significance the plaza was declared a state monument in 1957 and then listed on the National Register as a historical landmark in 1985.

A large plaque at one end of the plaza commemorates the flag raising. It reads: "The national flag will give protection to all persons who properly seek it. Criminals and other evil persons who seek to attain their ends by violent means and in violation of the known laws will find neither shelter nor protection under its ample folds."

A Time to Call It Quits

Mogollon

According to the unofficial town timepiece, it's always 4 o'clock in Mogollon. It's been that way for decades, ever since someone painted a giant pocket watch on the large rock that stands at the entrance of this former boomtown.

Since it's painted on a rock instead of a flat surface, the clock sort of resembles something Salvador Dalí might have done. But the hands are straight and the time is definitely 4 o'clock, which means that the timepiece is accurate at least twice in every 24-hour span.

★ ★

There are two stories about how it got there. One says it was painted in 1974 after the movie *My Name Is Nobody* was filmed in the area. The spaghetti Western spoof starred Henry Fonda and Terrence Hill as gunfighters.

But the more realistic version is that the clock was painted in 1942 when the mines closed due to lack of manpower and the miners put it there to commemorate their last shift.

Clock-watchers will find the good times in Mogollon, northwest of the Gila Wilderness Area about 60 miles north of Silver City on Highway 211, then 4 miles east on Highway 159. About 2,000 people lived there back in 1909, but today there are less than twenty-five permanent residents. And they all pronounce the name "muggy-yohn."

Just Desserts in the High Desert
Pie Town

Almost half the business places in this community are involved in the manufacture and distribution of pies. Percentage-wise, this is an impressive statistic. But the impact of pastry making gets slightly diluted in the face of this reality: There are only five business places in town, and one of them is the Post Office. And the listed population is seventy.

The place got its name around 1922 when Clyde Norman filed a gold-mining claim in the immediate area, situated at 8,000 feet above sea level and straddling the Continental Divide. He needed operating capital so he opened a small store where he sold supplies and other items, and he called it "Norman's Place." Then he tried peddling his homemade doughnuts but the coffee-dunkers who passed through weren't impressed. So Norman came up with a few variations of his mother's recipes and began baking pies. They were an instant success. People from all over Catron County motored over to his establishment to snarf up what they called "those great pies of Norman's."

Elated, Norman changed the name of his business to "Pie Town" and it's been that way ever since.

Today, the Daily Pie Cafe and the Pie-O-Neer Cafe carry on the tradition. Both establishments bake their pies every day, and they include such basics as apple, peach, and cherry, plus a few improvisations like cranberry-cherry. Both establishments participate in the annual Pie Festival, which features horny-toad races, arts, crafts, music, and, of course, pie-eating contests.

The town is located on US 60, about halfway between Datil and Quemado. The pie stores are on both sides of the highway, about ¼ mile from each other. For more information, log on to www.pietown .com.

Lightning Up the Sky
Quemado

In a way it seems only natural that Walter De Maria would select Quemado for his art project because *quemado* is the Spanish word for "burned" and De Maria works with lightning rods.

De Maria, an American sculptor, created *The Lightning Field,* a work of land art in a remote area of the high desert, in 1977. It's not like anything you'll ever find in a museum or gallery or probably any place else in the world because it consists of 400 polished stainless steel poles installed in a one square kilometer grid array. The poles are 2 inches in diameter and more than 20 feet tall. They're spaced 220 feet apart and their pointed tips define a horizontal plane, so it's a sculpture to be walked into as well as looked at.

Visitors are urged to spend an entire day there, if possible, so they can view the work by wandering through it at both sunrise and sunset. The Dia Art Foundation, which commissioned and maintains the project, also provides overnight lodging near the site.

But those who fork over the rather steep entry fee ($250 in July and August, $150 per head at other times) aren't guaranteed a lightning show. The literature describing the work notes that it "does not depend on the occurrence of lightning but responds to many more subtle conditions of its environment."

★ ★

Quemado is on US 60 about 25 miles east of the Arizona state line. A large white building on the north side of the main street bears a Dia Art Foundation sign but there's rarely anyone there. However, lightning chasers and steel-pole fans will find more information at www.lightningfield.org or call (505) 898-3335. But don't bother to take a camera; they don't allow photography.

A Lawman's Long Day
Reserve

When the subject turns to the matter of putting in a long, hard day on the job, the name of Elfego Baca should be included in the discussion. He became a legend in 1884 for doing what had to be done, no matter how long it took.

Reserve was known as San Francisco Plaza back then and the cowboys who ran the town made their own rules, so it was a rather lawless place. Baca was a sheriff's deputy who, although unauthorized to do so, rode into the town intending to bring some law and order to a rowdy place filled with rowdy cowboys who got most of their rowdiness from whiskey bottles. When Baca arrested one of the rowdies, he was immediately accosted by several armed cowboys who demanded the release of their good ol' drinkin' pardner. He refused, the rowdies got rowdier, and Baca and his prisoner were forced to take refuge in a small hut made of wood and mud.

For the next thirty-seven hours, the lawman and the captured rowdy had to lie flat on the mud floor, surrounded by as many as eighty cowboys determined to rescue their friend. Although an estimated 4,000 rounds were fired at him, Baca emerged unharmed. But four of his attackers were dead.

Ironically, Baca was arrested and returned to Socorro where he was charged with murder. He was acquitted and later became mayor of Socorro.

Today, most residents of Reserve don't make much of a fuss about the incident. But local businessman Henry Martinez thinks it should

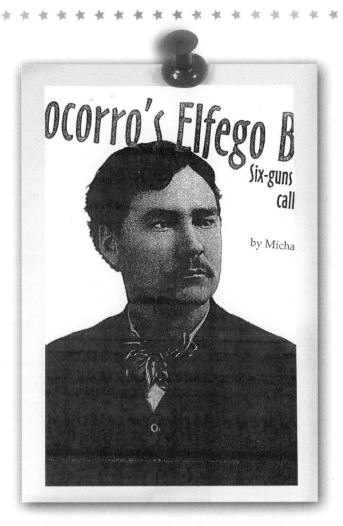

ocorro's Elfego B

Six-guns call

by Micha

Elfego Baca spent more than 30 hours trapped
by gunfighters, but he got his man.

be more than a footnote, so he spearheaded a drive to create and
erect a life-size bronze sculpture of Baca with his six-gun drawn. It
was dedicated in May 2008 and now stands in the town plaza, right
where the mud hut used to be. Martinez is also trying to establish a
museum to commemorate what will probably go down in history as
the Old West's longest shoot-out.

Reserve is about 65 miles southwest of Datil on Highway 12.

★ ★

The Little Burger That Could

San Antonio

According to the most recent census, there are 458 permanent residents living here, so it's rather improbable that anything in town is worthy of nationwide acclaim.

But there it is, in big letters on the sign in front of the Buckhorn Tavern: "No. 7 in America."

There isn't enough room on the sign to explain that the designation applies to the green-chile and cheese hamburger that owner Bob Olguin whips up, nor the bar itself. The honor came in 2007 when *GQ* sent reporters across the country in search of "the 20 hamburgers you have to eat before you die."

One of writers had been tipped off about Olguin's masterpiece by a *New York Times* reporter who had been in the area earlier on a different story and wrote a sidebar about the Buckhorn cuisine. The *GQ* staffer took his advice, stopped for a burger, and declared that it was "spectacularly tasty and emotionally coherent," worthy of the number seven ranking. He also noted that "the chiles, onions, mustard and cheese all battle to a spectacular draw" and that "basically, it's too much of everything on a bun."

Although honored and perhaps even a bit flattered by the attention, Olguin said the ranking should have been even higher because his is the only green chile cheeseburger on the list. But it's still good enough to get him an appearance on the Food Network. He creates his masterpieces in the same building his father, Manny, built as a bar and restaurant in 1943.

The assessment appeared in the May 2007 edition of *GQ*. Those who can't find a copy of that issue can read the one hanging on the east wall of the Buckhorn or do a search on the *GQ* website.

Getting hungry? The Buckhorn sits on the west edge of town on the south side of Highway 380, call (505) 835-4423. Or just slide on in by taking exit 139 off I-25 and heading straight east into town.

★ ★

You Were Born WHERE???!!!

San Antonio

Conrad Hilton—yes, *that* Conrad Hilton—was born and raised here, but only a few traces of his legacy are still around, including some ruins where the family's restaurant once stood and the front bar from the restaurant, which now sits in the Owl Bar and restaurant down the street. But a few old-timers who still claim to remember him, even though he left town at an early age to join the military and then eventually settled in Texas, where he built his first hotel.

And although he became richer and more famous than any of his boyhood cronies and spawned a family of heirs destined to become tabloid fodder, Hilton is still considered a hometown boy, as evidenced by this story that circulates among the populace:

Later in his life, Hilton was to be honored with a sort of "Key to Texas" due to his success as a businessman and a native-born Texan. All the plans were made for a big bash, but on the night before the presentation, someone pointed out that he had been born in the San Antonio in New Mexico, not the one in Texas. So, the story goes, somebody called Hilton and frantically pleaded, "Please, oh please, tell me you were born in Texas."

Unfortunately, for the sake of a good story, nobody recorded Hilton's response and he got the award regardless of his birthplace.

Planning Way, Way Ahead

Sierra County

Sir Richard Branson's passion for in space travel arose when he watched the Apollo moon landings in the late 1960s. And now aeronautics have made him rich so he can afford it. Branson has selected a piece of New Mexico desert to take his interest to its highest level—outer space travel for the common man.

In 2007 voters in Dona Ana County approved a gross receipts tax to help build the Spaceport America, a multi-million dollar project approved and spearheaded by the New Mexico Space Authority and headquarters for Branson's Virgin Galactic operation. Supporters envision launch pads and huge runways and expect thrill seekers of the highest order to flock to the site to blast off, spend six minutes in space, and see Earth from a vantage point formerly visited only by astronauts.

The Spaceport is already heralded as "one gateway in a community of gateways built not only in the United States but globally." The advance publicity also notes that someday, if all goes as planned, suborbital craft will jump from spaceport to spaceport and become an enterprise that will support vacation travelers, especially those who seek out-of-this-world experiences. Already in the works are plans for a similar venture near Van Horn, Texas, and a space hotel above Europe.

Construction of seven spaceships started about two years ago, and if all goes as planned, commercial space travel will become a reality in 2009. As of June 2007, there were already 70,000 potential space-persons registered to make the trip. And some have already made the down payment on the $200,000 round trip fare. For obvious reasons, they won't be selling the less expensive one-way tickets.

Although the voters in Dona Ana County approved the tax that will help fund the venture by a mere 240 votes out of 18,000 cast, the 100,000 square foot facility will be located in Sierra County near Upham, a non-populated area off I-25, 42 miles north of Las Cruces and 30 miles east of Truth or Consequences, on the perimeter of the White Sands Missile Range.

Scotty Finally Got to Outer Space
Sierra County

For years, at regular intervals on commercial television and later at unspecified times on those channels that continuously show reruns, James Doohan was part of the crew assigned to "boldly go where no man has gone before."

Doohan was the actor who portrayed Chief Engineer Montgomery "Scotty" Scott in the original *Star Trek* series in which the USS *Enterprise* made regular stops at faraway galaxies with strange-sounding names.

It was all make-believe, of course. But Scotty eventually did get to outer space. Two years after his death in 2005, seven grams of his ashes were placed into a capsule and launched on the SpaceLoft XL rocket from the area that will eventually become New Mexico's Spaceport America.

The rocket briefly entered outer space during a four-minute suborbital flight and then parachuted back to Earth with its unusual cargo intact. The craft also carried the ashes of Mercury astronaut Gordon Cooper, John Meredith Lucas, a writer for the original *Star Trek* series, and 200 others.

The remains of the 203 people were sealed in specially made metal capsules that were designed to survive the rigors of space flight. Once recovered, the cylinders were mounted on plaques and presented to the families.

It was the first rocket successfully launched into space from the Spaceport. The payload landed in rocky, steep canyons in the San Andres Mountains on the White Sands Missile Range. Although it took 20 days for crews to locate the containers, planners said it landed right where they had intended.

So everything went as planned, which must have been a relief for Scotty's soul because he didn't have to worry about anything going wrong with "my bairns" (children), as so frequently happened on TV.

Doesn't It Get Lonesome Out There?

Sierra County

The landscape along I-25 between Truth or Consequences and Socorro is pretty much flat, so flat that a great big brown thing sticking out of the ground draws some instant attention. And as it turns out, the thing is well worth making a side trip to check it out.

★ ★

Made of colored stone and rusted steel and rising about 20 feet above the flatlands, it's just sitting there, all by itself, on a lonely road that appears to wander off into the distance with no destination in sight. As so often happens, however, such an initial assumption is way off the mark.

The big brown thing is actually a sculpture titled *Camino del Sue- nos,* Spanish for "Road of Dreams." Greg Reiche, the sculptor, used large quantities of steel and stone to create the work, which serves as a marker to indicate that the El Camino Real International Heritage Center is 5 miles ahead.

The center also sits alone in the high wind-swept desert and is also definitely worth a visit. It traces the history of El Camino Real de Tierra Adentro (the Royal Road to the Interior), a 1,500-mile route that ran from Mexico City to Santa Fe, and is one of the most important lega- cies of the Spanish settlers who arrived around 1598.

The facility recounts the long and perilous journey through the use of exhibits, programs, artifacts, arts, and devotional items, many of them displayed in state-of-the-art showcases that depict the hard- ships the weary travelers encountered along the way.

To get to both sculpture and center, take exit 115 off I-25, about halfway between Truth or Consequences and Socorro, then take the frontage road and follow the signs. For more information, visit www .elcaminoreal.org or call (575) 834-3600.

A New House for Old Billy

Silver City

At one time, before he became the infamous desperado known as Billy the Kid, Billy Antrim was known around here simply as William Antrim's stepson. Antrim married Billy's mother, Catherine McCarty, and the family took up residence in a log cabin that sat where the Silver City Visitors Center is now located.

The cabin was washed away by a flood that swept through the heart of downtown on June 21, 1895. The flood, described as "an

immense wall of rolling water, 12 feet high and 300 feet wide,"
wiped out the entire business district and turned the main street into
a giant ditch about 35 feet deep.

The town was hit with more flooding in 1902, 1910, 1915, and
1925 so the gulch was never filled in. The main shopping center was
moved a block away and in the 1930s, the Civilian Conservation
Corps built dams across the oft-flooded gully. Today it's green and
lush and known as Big Ditch Park.

But there's a new cabin on the original site now, thanks to the
freckle-faced make-believe offspring of a make-believe sheriff.

Movie director Ron Howard, who played Sheriff Andy Taylor's son
Opie several years ago in *The Andy Griffith Show* television series,
had a replica of the cabin built for use in *The Missing,* a 2003 Western thriller set in New Mexico and starring Cate Blanchett and Tommy
Lee Jones. When the filming was over, Howard donated the cabin to
the city to give tourists "a flavor of frontier times."

The visitor center is at 201 North Hudson Street (Highway 90), and
the phone is (800) 548-9378.

Were Those Really Little Green Men?

Socorro

Like several other towns in New Mexico, Socorro claims it was once
the site of a UFO sighting. Unlike most others this one came from an
unusually reliable source—a local policeman.

It happened on April 24, 1946. Sgt. Lonnie Zamora, the cop, was
chasing a speeder on the outskirts when he heard a roar emitting
from behind a nearby hill. Zamora initially thought the noise was an
explosion at a dynamite shack so he drove over the hill to check it
out.

What he saw, he later claimed, was a metallic oval-shaped object
with a strange symbol on it. He also said he saw two small manlike
creatures wearing what looked like white coveralls, walking around
the object. Zamora said that when the things spotted him, they

jumped into their "spacecraft" and took off with a roar that shook his police car.

After Zamora radioed for assistance, Sgt. M. S. Chavez of the New Mexico State Police arrived at the scene and said the Socorro lawman looked terrified. He also noted that bushes in the area were burned and saw what he said were strange scoop marks in the ground.

Project Blue Book, the U.S. Air Force's official UFO study unit, sent investigators to Socorro. They interviewed both principals and concluded that "there is no doubt that Lonnie Zamora saw an object which left quite an impression on him" and then added that "there is no question about Zamora's reliability."

UFO skeptics weren't buying his claims, however. One said it was either a prank staged by local teenagers or a very large dust devil. Others said it was an elaborate hoax, designed to bring tourists to the area. But researchers also found flaws in their assumptions.

Zamora still lives in Socorro but refuses to talk about the incident, even though it has become a part of area folklore.

Imagine What Tiger Would Have Shot
Socorro

Mike Stanley, who lives and works here, once shot thirty-five under par on a local golf layout. Tiger Woods never shot a score that low. Neither did Sam Snead or Ben Hogan or even Arnie Palmer.

But it gets even better.

Stanley did it on one hole.

New Mexico's Kathy Whitworth never did that. Neither did Phil Mickelson or Jack Nicklaus in his prime. The best any of them ever got on one hole was an eagle, a mere two under par.

Naturally, that's a bit curious and, naturally, it wasn't regulation golf. Stanley did it while participating in the Elfego Baca Golf Shootout, an annual event that starts at the top of Socorro Peak and finishes at the bottom of the mountain. It's named after Elfego Baca, the lawman who once survived a thirty-seven-hour gun battle and later became mayor of Socorro.

The hole is about 2½ miles long and it's par 50. The only redeeming quality is that it's all downhill. Only ten golfers are allowed to participate every year. Each player is given ten specially marked golf balls and three spotters. The golfers tee off from the top of the peak, at about 7,500 feet above sea level, and whack their way down the mountain. They send their spotters well ahead and aim for them so they can find the balls, but the golfers don't get penalized if they, or their spotters, lose one in the rocky canyons.

When they get to the bottom, the survivors must still be playing with one of the original golf balls and then must knock it into a 50-foot circle that constitutes the golf hole.

Stanley won or tied for the shootout title eighteen times before retiring. His longest drive rolled 650 yards down the mountainside, and his lowest total was fifteen. And that's 35 under par.

Most golfers will never be able to accomplish that.

Not even when they keep their own score.

A Brief Walk through History
Socorro

Not only does Socorro have the longest golf hole in the world, but on the other end of the spectrum, it also boasts what is probably the world's (or, at least, this nation's) shortest scenic byway. Where other byways wander over mountaintops, down into canyons, and across glacier fields, Socorro's pretty much stays right at home.

Its name is almost as long as the route. It's known as the Socorro Historical District Scenic Byway and it starts in the plaza right in the heart of the city. It goes past old churches that trace their beginnings back to 1628, and past the splendid San Miguel Mission, built in 1891 on the site of the original mission. The walkway also takes visitors to museums that display artifacts from the town's mining heritage and passes several examples of early Spanish architecture.

★ ★

One of the twenty-two stops is in front of the Socorro City Hall, where the humble beginnings of the city have been captured in a huge circular bronze sculpture known as *The Socorro Wheel of History.* The wheel memorializes the town's earliest settlers, going all the way back to 1598 when explorer Don Juan de Oñate and his weary men were given food and shelter. In gratitude, they named the settlement "Socorro," Spanish for "succor."

The history of Socorro is told in the round on this wheel along the city's scenic byway.

The really good thing this scenic byway is that those in a historical hurry can drive past every stop in about thirty minutes because the route covers only 2.9 miles.

Although it's doubtful that anyone will ever get lost along the way, maps are available at the Socorro Heritage and Visitors Center on the north side of Socorro Plaza a block south of US 60. For more information, call (505) 835-0424 or log onto www.socorro-nm.com.

A Side Effect of Something Awful
Socorro

On July 16, 1945, at 5:29 a.m., the sky around Socorro was literally set afire when the United States tested the world's first atomic bomb in an experiment code-named "Trinity." It ushered in the atomic age, and the verbal battle over whether it was a good thing or a bad thing still rages.

After the blast scientists inspecting Ground Zero discovered that the area's sandy surface was pitted with a green, glassy solid substance. The men of science deduced that the green color was due to the iron content of the sand, then named the formation "trinitite."

The exact process of creating trinitite is still being debated. An original theory said it was formed when the intense heat of the explosion made contact with the sand below. But in 2005 Robert Hermes and William Strickfaden, scientists from the Los Alamos National Lab (where the atomic bomb had been designed and developed), concluded that the sand must have been scooped up into the fireball before it was melted by the intense heat (14,710 degrees Fahrenheit). The molten glass then fell as droplets, creating small pools of trinitite.

To date nobody has figured out a practical use for the material. Some of it is still lying around on the ground, but viewing it can be a challenge because visitors are allowed on the site only during one-day open houses held every April and October.

Rock hounds and others can get more information by visiting www.wsmr.army.mil or by calling (505) 678-1134. Look, but don't take: It's illegal to remove trinitite.

Go Ahead, We're Listening
Socorro County

While driving along US 60 west of Socorro, a series of huge white things that look like giant television receptors suddenly loom on the horizon. They are part of a scientific experiment known as the Very Large Array. But those who don't know about the Very Large Array will frequently stop, stare, gasp, and make such perceptive comments as "Judging from the size of those dishes, I imagine they get good TV reception out here." And, not infrequently, "If they laid them on the ground, I bet those things would hold a lot of beer."

But although the observations are astute, the huge saucerlike devices have nothing to do with sitcoms, instant replays, brews, or

★ ★

The Very Large Array has been listening to outer space for more than 25 years.

soap operas. Instead, they're part of the National Radio Astronomy Observatory's Very Large Array, a huge composite radio telescope that listens for and captures radio waves from outer space.

The array consists of twenty-seven dish-shaped antennas, each measuring 82 feet across and weighing 230 tons. They are arranged in a Y-shaped configuration on tracks along a trio of 13-mile stretches on the Plains of San Agustin. The data from the dishes is combined electronically to give the resolution of an antenna 22 miles across.

While those who see it for the first time might have visions of science fiction and alien invasions, the complex is old news to area residents because it has been there for more than twenty-five years.

Since its inception the VLA has made more scientific discoveries than any other ground-based telescope in history. The giant platters have also starred in the Jodie Foster movie *Contact* and several documentaries. But they haven't heard from anyone trying to relocate from Venus.

The Visitor Center is open daily and guided tours are conducted twice per year. To get there, take US 60 west of Socorro for 52 miles, then turn south on Highway 52 for two miles to the VLA access road. For details, log on to www.vla.nrao.edu or contact the education office at (505) 835-7243.

A Real Whoosher

Three Rivers

The Three Rivers Petroglyph Site itself isn't a genuine curiosity because it's quite similar to hundreds of others spread across the nation—a large area with a lot of boulders marked with symbols and drawings that were chiseled and pecked into rocks centuries ago by native tribesmen.

But a few items make it worth inclusion. One is the name. There are no rivers in the area. And according to the site manager, there never were rivers anywhere near the area. There may have been three streams around here a long time ago, he said. But Three Rivers is much easier to pronounce than Three Streams, which could turn out to be a tongue-twister after a long day of looking at petroglyphs.

All that nomenclature nonsense aside, the site is most impressive and worth stopping at because there are more than 21,000 petroglyphs on the grounds, and each has been recorded by the Archaeological Society of New Mexico's Rock Art Recording Field. The endeavor took more than six years.

And now for the Really Big Curiosity that'll blow you away. Literally.

Male visitors who use the toilet facility should be aware of "Xcelerator." There are no paper towels in the men's restroom so those who go there must rely on "Xcelerator," a blow dryer attached to a wall. It is like none other. Turn it on and a tornado-like gust of air

★ ★

comes roaring out with a force so strong that it doesn't merely blow the moisture away; it blasts it off. The gale is so powerful it'll clean your knuckles, scrape the dirt from underneath your fingernails, and put a nice shine on your hiking boots.

Hurricane fans and those in need of a good air-drying will find the petroglyph site on Country Road 830 as it wanders about five miles east of a trading post called Three Rivers on US 54, north of Tularosa.

A Tribute to Good Ol' Ralph
Truth or Consequences

Those who remember the radio quiz shows of the 1930s and 1940s will easily make the connection between the programs and how this town got such a long name because one of the shows was *Truth or Consequences,* hosted by Ralph Edwards.

The program went on the airwaves in 1940 and was so success-ful that in 1950, Edwards announced that he was looking for a town that would change its name to Truth or Consequences in honor of the program's tenth anniversary.

Hot Springs, New Mexico, was among the cities, towns, and vil-lages that applied, and that particular application intrigued Edwards enough that he sent his producer out to the flatlands of Sierra County to check it out. The producer was impressed with the hot springs that gave the city its original name, so he turned in a favor-able report. Edwards agreed, the deal was made, and on March 21, 1950, by a vote of 1,294 to 295, the citizenry approved the name change. The next day, Edwards broadcast his show from there as the city held its first Truth or Consequences Fiesta.

Edwards returned every year until 2000 to take part in the fiesta and thus became a city icon. He has a park, street, and auditorium named after him. A life-size bust of his personage sits in front of the civic center and a plaque honoring him hangs on an exterior wall of a museum. The nineteen-letter name (twenty-one if you count spaces as letters because they're about the same width) has survived for more than a half century despite attempts to change it back to Hot Springs. The issue has been put to a vote twice and lost both times by two-to-one margins.

But not everything went "T or C" (as the locals refer to it these days). The high school remains Hot Springs High and the athletic teams are nicknamed the Tigers. It's probably for the best. After all, think of the poor cheerleaders trying to rouse the crowd with "Go, fight, fight, you Truth or Consequences High School Ralphs!"

There's Little Joy in Being Joy
Truth or Consequences

If it weren't for the peculiar name, this community would probably be known and highly respected for its rather quirky artworks. They include a steer made of old boards and auto parts, a ceramic waterfall, giant flowers, and muralized water tanks.

The ceramic waterfall gurgles on the site of an original spring that once bubbled next to what is now the Geronimo Springs Museum in the heart of downtown. It's green and blue . . and red and yellow . . . and some other colors. They're all combined into a surrealistic spring/waterfall that cools the atmosphere of the high desert while representing the original name of the community—Palomas Springs.

A few blocks away, at the same Civic Center that houses the bust of Ralph Edwards, local artist Delmas Howe has painted huge flowers on the exterior panels. They are brilliantly colored works, each measuring 6 feet tall by 3 feet wide and representing desert flora in magnificent magnification.

The Sierra County Arts Council commissioned Anthony Pennock to convert the city's two water tanks into works of art, and he performed his assigned task admirably, considering that his canvas was circular, steel, and more than 30 feet high. He adorned them with Western scenes that reflect the area's heritage. Both are highly visible because water storage tanks, by their very nature, are usually placed on higher elevations and these are no exception to that law of gravity.

★ ★

The most unusual artwork, however, is Joy the Steer. It sits in a parking lot next to the State National Bank on the corner of Pershing and Main, and it's made of cedar planks, car parts, and other discarded items. The creature takes its name from the word "joy" cast into the grill of an old wood-burning stove that the artist, R. William Winkler, scavenged from a cattle ranch along Percha Creek and integrated into his creation.

There is ongoing discussion about the name. Winkler says it could mean something like, "Oh joy! Prime rib tonight!" But others say it's an oxymoron. After all, they say, considering the circumstances required to create a steer, what joy can there be in becoming one?

The Wall That Heals
Truth or Consequences

The "Wall" is 240 feet long and sits on the southwestern outskirts of the city at 996 South Broadway. The official name is rather long—the Truth or Consequences Vietnam Veterans Memorial Park and Museum—but a monument of this caliber deserves a lengthy designation.

The wall is a half-scale replica of the Vietnam Veterans Memorial in Washington, D.C., designed by Maya Ying Lin. Like the original this version lists the names of 57,939 service men and women who were killed or went missing in action during that conflict. The difference is that the names on the actual memorial are carved into marble; those on this version are etched into metal panels.

Four such replicas were designed to travel around the country and overseas. This one was created in 1999 and shipped all the way to Ireland where it was displayed at Cork, Dublin, and Limerick in the Irish Republic and Belfast in Northern Ireland. After that journey, the wall was acquired by the city and placed at its current site in the park, where it was dedicated on Nov. 7, 2003. Now, it is commonly referred to as "the wall that heals."

The names are listed chronologically, starting in the center with the year 1959 and flowing to the right. They pick up again at the far left and flow back to the center, to the year 1975.

★ ★

But there's more to the park. Behind the primary attraction are 16 stone markers topped with marble slabs, standing in recognition of all the armed conflicts in which this nation has been involved, starting with the Revolutionary War. Fifteen of the markers are engraved with brief histories of the bloody encounters. The sixteenth slab sits blank, waiting for the next war to end.

No Lumber Shortage Here

Tularosa

Jan Clayton was born here. It was way back in 1917 and she never got to be real famous, but it's still one of the community's claims to fame. That and the big trees.

Clayton was an actress who once portrayed Julie Jordan in a Broadway production of *Carousel.* She also married and divorced B Western actor Russell Hayden and drove a Rolls-Royce with a personalized license plate that said "Jan Who." And she appeared in a variety of television shows, including *The Love Boat* and *Streets of San Francisco,* before her death in 1983.

But the big trees are still here. One is New Mexico's largest sycamore, a 108-footer that towers over the corner of Seventh Street and Encino. Planted in 1941, it now measures more than 4 feet in diameter. A plaque attached to the trunk gives the giant's history.

Down the road a block, at Sixth and Encino, a humungous three-trunked cottonwood tree takes up a whole lot of space in somebody's front yard. It measures more than 6 feet in diameter, which means it would take several people to encircle it, providing they have long arms. It also would seem to be in the wrong town. It should be in Alamogordo, which is Spanish for "fat cottonwood."

But if that's not enough to merit a stop, consider this: Two of the town's more popular eateries are the Donkey Dust Cafe and Yum Yum's Donut Shop.

Tularosa is 79 miles south of Albuquerque on I-25.

★ ★

No Place for Spelling Sissies

There's not much of anything in Zuzax even though there's a Zuzax exit off Interstate 40 about 11 miles east of Albuquerque. In fact, there never was much of anything in Zuzax, not even when it came into existence around 1956. Herman Ardans, a quick-thinking entrepreneur, opened a curio shop on old Route 66 and made up the name Zuzax because it was so weird that it would attract the attention of passersby. Besides that, it would also be the last name listed in the telephone book. But when asked where the name came from, Ardans facetiously said it referred to the Zuzax Indians.

Ardans also installed a chairlift that took tourists to the top of a small hill behind his store. Today, there's only a gas station and convenience store on the original site, but several housing subdivisions have sprung up in the surrounding area.

And now, in some sort of fulfillment of Ardans's wishes, Zuzax is the last name listed in Robert Julyan's monumental work titled *The Place Names of New Mexico*.

It's All about the Name

White Sands National Monument

For anyone who's ever spent a winter in snow country, driving through White Sands National Monument can be a chilling experience because it's a world of white. The ground is white, the hills are white, all the vegetation is covered with white, and there are kids sliding down the white slopes. And the roads have to be bladed to keep them open, just like North Dakota in January.

But it's not snow; it's gypsum. This, the Tularosa Basin, is the world's largest gypsum dune field, engulfing 275 square miles of the Chihuahuan Desert. The mineral was deposited at the bottom of a shallow sea that covered the area about 250 million years ago. Eventually converted into stone, the gypsum-bearing marine deposits were raised up into a giant dome at the same time the Rocky Mountains were forming, seventy million years ago. About ten million years ago, the center of the dome began to cave in and created the basin.

Gypsum, a hydrous form of calcium sulfate, is rarely found in the form of sand because it is water soluble. Rain and snow from the surrounding mountains dissolve gypsum from the rocks and carry it into the basin. But no waterways drain the basin and rainfall in the area is measured in fractions, so the gypsum and other sediments are trapped there. If it did rain on a regular basis, the water would dissolve the stuff and carry it away to a river or stream. But it doesn't, so the gypsum stays. Just the way Nature intended.

The gypsum sand is even more of a rarity because most sand is composed of quartz instead of calcium sulfate. But gypsum sand is called "sand" anyway. Probably because it sounds better. Think about it. Would tourists actually stop at the White Gypsum National Monument? Would anyone really want to go sunbathing on a "gyp-summy beach"?

White Sands is located on US 70 about 12 miles south of Alamogordo. Those who like to play in the snow when it's warm outside can get more information by logging on to www.nps.gov/whsa or call (575) 479-6124.

index

index

index

index

about the author

Sam Lowe has been looking at the world in a slightly obtuse fashion for more than forty years, first as a newspaper columnist and now as a freelance writer. He has written countless travel stories and five other books. He has also wing-walked on top of an airplane, singled off Hall of Fame pitcher Juan Marichal, been stranded in Zambia for ten days, impersonated a wax dummy, eaten fifty-seven baby back ribs at one sitting, and failed in several attempts to either win the lottery or find the Lost Dutchman gold mine. Lowe lives in Phoenix with Lyn and Zach, a beautiful wife and faithful dog, respectively.